CAMPING AND RVING 101: THE ULTIMATE BEGINNERS GUIDE

GEAR, CAMPSITE SETUP, HOOKUPS, NAVIGATION, AND MORE FOR RVS AND TENTING

D.K. JACKSON

CONTENTS

Introduction   5

1. INTRODUCTION TO CAMPING AND RVING   9
   The Camping and RV Lifestyle   10
   Selecting Quality Gear   15

2. FINANCING YOUR RV AND CAMPING
   ADVENTURES   21
   Financing Options for Purchasing an RV   24
   Budgeting Tips for Camping Trips and Long-Term
   Travel   27

3. CHOOSING THE RIGHT RV OR TENT   35
   Types of RVs: Class A, B, C, and Travel Trailers   35
   Choosing the Right Tent for Your Needs   44

4. SETTING UP YOUR CAMPSITE   61
   Step-By-Step Guide to Setting up an RV or Tent   62
   How to Select the Perfect Campsite   67
   Campground Etiquette   72

5. RV HOOKUPS AND UTILITIES   77
   Electricity, Water, and Sewage Hookups   77
   Troubleshooting Common Utility Issues   88

6. NAVIGATING AND TRAVEL PLANNING   95
   Planning Your Route: Tools and Tips   95
   Navigating with an RV or While Towing   106
   Best Practices for Safe and Enjoyable Travel   110

7. MAINTENANCE, STORAGE, AND SECURITY   115
   Regular RV Maintenance Tips   116
   Seasonal Maintenance: Pre-Season and Off-Season
   Checks   125

How to Store Your RV or Camping Gear 129
Keeping Your Campsite and Belongings Secure 135

8. ADVANCED TIPS AND HACKS FOR SEASONED
RVERS 141
Upgrading Your RV Experience 143
Innovative Camping Hacks 152
Engaging with the RV and Camping Community 159
Embracing Life on the Road 161

Conclusion 165
Bonus Checklist 167
References 171

INTRODUCTION

The excitement of planning the ultimate camping adventure—envisioning the crackling campfire, the peaceful surroundings, and the thrill of outdoor freedom. You meticulously plan every detail, only to find yourself standing on a campsite surrounded by a chaotic mess of unassembled gear. It's a bit like trying to solve a puzzle, but the pieces aren't exactly cooperating as you'd expect.

The transition from the excitement of planning to the daunting reality of gear assembly is something we've all been through. It's that moment where the idyllic scenes in your mind collide with the practical challenges on the ground. The serene campfire setting you imagined suddenly feels overshadowed by the logistics of poles and wires scattered around you.

But fear not! The seemingly chaotic assembly phase is just a fleeting prelude to the genuine enchantment awaiting you. Once you've conquered the setup with poles in place and wires untangled, you'll find yourself immersed in the serene beauty of nature, bathed in the warmth of a crackling fire beneath a celestial canopy of stars.

Setting up camp or maneuvering an RV often feels like stepping into a whirlwind of uncertainty. What initially exudes peaceful nature vibes suddenly transforms into a race against time. Poles, stakes, and ropes accumulate, creating a perplexing puzzle where you're left wondering how each piece fits into the grand tent assembly. It's like deciphering a riddle while juggling an entire camping store's worth of gear.

And then there's the world of RVing—an entirely new realm to conquer. You take the wheel with the excitement of conquering the open road, only to be confronted with perplexing questions about dumping stations and electrical hookups. Your confidence wavers and the once thrilling anticipation of the trip seems to deflate as swiftly as air from a subpar air mattress.

That initial moment of uncertainty, caught in the whirlwind of setting up camp or maneuvering an RV, can leave you feeling like you're in a tailspin. Questions like where each part goes and why hammering in a single stake feels like a Herculean task become the soundtrack to your initiation into the camping world.

But here's the reassuring truth: that initial panic is merely a passing storm. Once you grasp the intricacies, decipher the tent's secret language, or understand the RV's quirky systems, everything falls into place. Suddenly, you find yourself fireside, surrounded by nature's beauty, relishing the peace and quiet, and chuckling at those initial struggles. It's all part of the adventure!

Consider this guide your personal roadmap to the vast camping and RVing universe—a genie in a bottle ready to whisk away the stress and confusion. We've got your back, untangling those intricate setup instructions and translating camping jargon into plain English. Soon enough, you'll master the art of setting up camp with finesse, toasting s'mores like a pro, and nestling into your sleeping bag beneath a star-studded sky.

Think of us as your camping gurus, here to ensure your outdoor adventures are nothing short of spectacular. We're like your best pals, guiding you through the wilderness, sharing insider tips, and cheering you on as you conquer the camping world.

So, wave goodbye to those panic-stricken moments. You're stepping into a world teeming with unforgettable camping experiences. Ready to embrace nature like never before? Dive right in! Just a fair warning... those s'mores? They're addictively delicious!

CHAPTER 1

INTRODUCTION TO CAMPING AND RVING

Have you noticed how, in the past couple of decades, there's been this crazy surge in people getting into camping and RVing? Like, seriously, RV ownership has shot up by a whopping 62%!

But why the sudden boom?

Well, first off, camping and RVing are like the ultimate freedom passes. They're your ticket to break out of the daily grind, ditch the office walls for starry skies, and trade city chaos for wild, untamed nature. It's like having your own home on wheels, where the journey itself becomes your kick-ass destination.

And hey, in a world where we're always glued to screens and bombarded by notifications, camping and RVing are a breath of fresh air—literally! Think sunsets instead of screens, bird songs instead of phone pings, and peace and quiet instead of stress. Nature's calling, and it's calling pretty darn loud!

But here's the cool thing—it's not just about finding solitude. When you hit those campgrounds, it's like stepping into a community of adventure seekers. Strangers become buddies over campfires and late-night stories under a sky packed with stars. It's like this unspoken bond we all share—our love for the great outdoors.

And let's not forget the thrill of it all! Camping and RVing are all about diving headfirst into the unknown, soaking in breathtaking views, and creating stories that'll stick with you forever. It's the ultimate promise of adventure—the kind that gets your heart racing and leaves you with stories to tell for a lifetime.

So, this whole camping and RVing explosion? It's not just about getting fancy vehicles and hitting the road. It's about a shift in how we live and experience life—a hunger for freedom, connections, and the rush of exploring. It's an invitation to join a movement where every mile is a new chapter in your epic adventure.

THE CAMPING AND RV LIFESTYLE

The Camping and RV Lifestyle is a tale woven from the fabric of time, spanning from its humble origins in the late 19th century to the thrilling modern-day adventures that captivate millions worldwide. What started as a means of survival and daring exploration has blossomed into an entire lifestyle, cherished by enthusiasts around the globe.

Back in the late 1800s, camping's roots stretched deep into the endeavors of intrepid explorers and pioneers. These trailblazers sought shelter, sustenance, and a deep connection with nature in the wild. It was a rugged and essential experience, laying the groundwork for what camping would become. This era marked the birth of organized camping—clubs and associations emerged, fostering camaraderie among those drawn to the great outdoors. They shared stories, wisdom, and a profound appreciation for the raw beauty of nature.

However, the landscape of camping and outdoor living truly transformed with the advent of recreational vehicles, fondly known as RVs. These vehicles represented a paradigm shift—a fusion of mobility and comfort that revolutionized outdoor living. In their early iterations, RVs were modest and utilitarian, yet they unlocked the spirit of adventure for countless individuals. Over time, these vehicles evolved into sophisticated, fully-equipped homes-on-wheels, complete with amenities rivaling those found in traditional residences. The evolution has been astounding, shaping the way people engage with the world outdoors.

The realm of camping and RVing today is as diverse as the landscapes they traverse. It spans a rich spectrum of experiences tailored to suit every adventurer's craving for exploration and freedom. It's not just about weekend getaways in national parks anymore, though those remain cherished adventures. There's a growing trend of individuals embracing the full-time RV lifestyle, where the road becomes home and every horizon is a new possibility. This diversity underscores the adaptability and versatility of this lifestyle, offering avenues for adventure and escape in ways that resonate deeply with the souls of explorers. Whether it's a temporary escape or a lifelong journey, camping and RVing offer a tapestry of experiences, each thread woven with the spirit of exploration and the quest for freedom. Plus, the camping lifestyle offers many awesome benefits. Let's dive deeper into why camping and RVing are way more than just pitching a tent or cruising in an RV. Think of it as your ultimate ticket to freedom, where the road becomes your canvas, waiting for your adventures to paint it with unforgettable moments.

1. Environmental awareness

Being immersed in natural settings fosters a deep appreciation for the environment. It allows you to witness firsthand the delicate balance of ecosystems and the impact of human actions. This heightened awareness often translates into adopting eco-friendly practices in daily life, such as reducing waste, conserving resources, and supporting conservation efforts.

2. Adventure and exploration

Camping is synonymous with adventure. Each trip offers a new frontier to explore, from serene lakeshores to majestic mountain peaks. It encourages a spirit of exploration and curiosity, igniting the thrill of discovering hidden trails, secret viewpoints, and breathtaking landscapes. The freedom to wander and uncover these hidden gems is an unparalleled adventure in itself.

3. Family bonding

Camping brings families closer by creating an environment free from distractions. Shared experiences like setting up camp, cooking meals together, and embarking on nature walks forge deeper connections. It's in these moments that families strengthen bonds, fostering communication, trust, and teamwork among members of all ages.

4. Creativity and resourcefulness

Camping often presents scenarios where quick thinking and resourcefulness become essential. Whether it's devising a makeshift shelter during unexpected rain or using natural elements for cooking, camping encourages inventive problem-solving. These moments of improvisation nurture creativity and adaptability, valuable skills applicable far beyond the campsite.

5. Mindful living

Disconnecting from the hustle of everyday life allows for mindfulness. In the tranquility of nature, one can fully absorb and appreciate the present moment—the rustling leaves, the melody of bird calls, the scent of pine. It's an opportunity to practice gratitude, reduce stress, and find peace in the simplicity of the present.

6. Physical activity and well-being

Camping inherently involves physical activities like hiking, swimming, or cycling. Engaging in these outdoor pursuits not only boosts physical fitness but also enhances mental well-being. The blend of fresh air, natural surroundings, and physical exertion leads to improved mood, reduced stress, and increased energy levels.

7. Cultural understanding

Traveling to various campsites exposes campers to diverse cultures, traditions, and ways of life. Whether it's learning about local customs from neighboring campers or exploring nearby towns, camping becomes a window to cultural exploration. It fosters an appreciation for diversity, broadening perspectives, and nurturing tolerance.

8. Unforgettable memories

Camping is a treasure trove of memorable experiences. Each trip brings moments that imprint themselves on the canvas of memory —a campfire conversation with newfound friends, watching shooting stars in the night sky, or simply witnessing the sunrise from a mountaintop. These experiences become stories that are recounted with fondness, shaping your personal narrative.

9. Problem-solving skills

Camping inevitably presents challenges that require quick thinking and problem-solving. Whether it's navigating rough terrain, fixing equipment issues, or adapting to changing weather, these situations hone problem-solving abilities and foster resilience. Overcoming these challenges strengthens confidence and adaptability.

10. Appreciation for simple living

Amidst the simplicity of camping, surrounded by the basics, individuals often gain a deeper appreciation for life's essentials. It's a reminder that happiness can be found in simple pleasures—a warm campfire, a starry night, or a heartfelt conversation. This appreciation tends to extend beyond the campsite, influencing attitudes toward materialism and promoting a more mindful approach to life.

These experiences aren't just about camping; they're about creating a life filled with adventures and stories that become a part of who you are. Each camping trip brings its own unique blend of experiences that enrich your life in countless ways.

SELECTING QUALITY GEAR

Finding the perfect balance between cost-effectiveness and durability is paramount when talking about camping gear. This balance ensures that the equipment you invest in not only fits your budget but also stands the test of various outdoor conditions, enhancing your overall camping experience.

For RV camping:

- **Leveling blocks:** These are saviors on uneven ground, ensuring your RV stays stable and you can set up camp without feeling like you're sleeping on a slant. Look for sturdy materials like high-density polyethylene. While cost-effective options exist, prioritize durability to ensure they withstand frequent use. Check weight limits to support your RV size. Investing in heavy-duty blocks may offer longevity.

- **Sewer hoses and connections:** An unglamorous but crucial item. They're the heroes for waste disposal and keeping your RV clean and fresh while on the road. Opt for hoses made of durable, crush-resistant materials like polyolefin. Ensure connections are leak-proof and made of robust materials for longevity. Balance cost with length and flexibility, aiming for a hose that suits your RV's setup without compromising quality.
- **Water hoses and filters:** Clean water is a non-negotiable. These ensure you have access to potable water wherever your adventure takes you. Seek hoses made of reinforced, lead-free materials for durability. Select filters with long-term use in mind, focusing on their filtration capacity and longevity.
- **Basic toolkit:** When Murphy's Law hits and something needs fixing, having a toolkit onboard lets you handle minor repairs and keep your journey rolling smoothly. Invest in a toolkit with durable tools made of corrosion-resistant materials. A balance between cost and quality is crucial for essential repairs.
- **Emergency kit:** It's like your safety net. First aid supplies, flashlights, extra batteries, and tools for those "just in case" moments. Ensure the kit includes high-quality first-aid supplies and reliable lighting sources. Focus on the quality of the included tools and supplies.
- **RV GPS or maps:** Getting lost might sound romantic, but not when you're trying to find a campground. These tools are your navigational compasses for safe travel. Consider GPS systems with updated maps and reliable navigation features. Opting for reputable brands ensures better accuracy and durability.

- **RV electrical adapters and surge protectors:** They're like shields for your RV's electrical systems, protecting them from power surges and ensuring you can plug in wherever you land. Prioritize surge protectors with solid safety ratings and durable construction. Balancing cost with safety features is vital for electrical equipment.

- **Fire extinguisher:** A must-have for safety. It's there for peace of mind in case things get heated in a different way than you intended. Choose fire extinguishers that meet safety standards and have sturdy construction. Ensure they are appropriate for RV use.

- **Awning lights or lanterns:** Picture-perfect ambiance around your RV at night. These provide cozy lighting for those evenings under the stars. Look for weather-resistant and long-lasting lighting options. Assess the quality of illumination offered against the price.

- **Camp chairs and table:** The ultimate outdoor comfort boost. Perfect for lounging or dining al fresco, these make your campsite feel like a home away from home. Invest in chairs and tables made of durable materials with suitable weight capacities. Balance quality and cost for long-term use.

For tent camping:

- **Tent:** Your portable shelter—make sure it suits your needs and the weather, creating a cozy haven for your camping adventure. Choose tents with robust materials and sturdy zippers for durability. Balancing cost with weather resistance is crucial.

- **Sleeping bags:** The cocoon for restful nights under the stars. They keep you warm and snug during your outdoor slumber party.
- **Portable stove or cooking equipment:** For your outdoor kitchen setup, these are essential for whipping up delicious meals and savoring the camping experience.
- **Lantern or flashlight with extra batteries:** When the sun sets, these become your guiding lights for nocturnal activities or just finding your way to the bathroom.
- **Camp kitchen supplies:** Your kitchen away from home. Utensils, cookware, and dishes—these essentials make meal prep and dining a breeze.

Prioritize materials known for durability while considering the cost-effectiveness of each item.

- **Camping chairs and table:** Comfort is key. These transform your camping spot into a cozy hangout for relaxing or sharing meals.
- **Campground map and navigation tools:** Your treasure map for exploring nature's wonders. These help you navigate trails and discover hidden gems.
- **Ground cover or tarp:** Protect your tent from moisture and wear, ensuring a dry and comfy sleeping space.
- **Sleeping pads or air mattresses:** These offer extra cushioning and insulation for a more restful sleep, adding a layer of comfort to your tent life.

- **Bug repellent and sunscreen:** Nature's essentials. These protect against pesky bugs and the sun's rays, ensuring you can enjoy the outdoors comfortably.

These essentials aren't just items on a checklist—they're the backbone of your camping experience, ensuring comfort, safety, and a smooth journey into the great outdoors. Remember, the specific gear you need might vary depending on your camping style, location, and personal preferences. Packing essentials while keeping in mind the activities you plan to engage in will ensure a more comfortable and enjoyable camping experience.

Wrapping up this chapter on gearing up for your camping adventure, let's talk money—because understanding the financial side of things is key to a stress-free trip. Whether you're rolling in an RV or setting up camp in a tent, having a grip on the financial aspects can make your experience smoother and more enjoyable. So, get ready to dive into the world of financing your RV and camping adventures. Understanding the ins and outs of costs, budgeting, and smart spending will be your compass to a worry-free journey. Stick around for the next chapter, where we'll unravel the financial complexities of RV ownership and camping to set you on the path to financial freedom on the road.

CHAPTER 2

FINANCING YOUR RV AND CAMPING ADVENTURES

When diving into the world of RV ownership and camping, it's easy to get bedazzled by the array of RV models and the promise of endless adventures on the open road. However, lurking beneath the excitement lies a myriad of costs that extend far beyond the initial price tag of your dream RV.

Sure, the sticker price might catch your eye first, but the real journey begins when you realize that owning an RV involves a comprehensive understanding of the expenses that come with it. It's like peeling back the layers of an onion—each one revealing a different aspect of the costs involved.

Firstly, let's talk about the RV itself. There's the upfront cost of purchasing the vehicle, which can vary immensely depending on the type, size, and features you desire. But that's just the tip of the iceberg. Consider the ongoing expenses such as insurance, maintenance, and storage fees. You'll want to safeguard your investment, and that means factoring in insurance premiums to protect against any unforeseen incidents on the road.

Maintenance is another significant aspect. Your RV is your home-on-wheels, and just like any home, it requires upkeep. Regular maintenance checks, engine servicing, and ensuring all systems are in top-notch condition are essential for a hassle-free journey. And let's not forget storage fees—unless you plan on parking it in your backyard, you'll need to budget for a safe and secure storage spot when you're not out adventuring.

Then come the operational costs. Think about the fuel—it's the lifeblood of your travels. Whether you're cruising down the highway or navigating winding mountain roads, fuel costs add up. And when you find that perfect spot to park your RV for a few nights, campground fees come into play. Some campgrounds offer luxurious amenities, but they often come with a price tag.

Upgrades and repairs? They're part and parcel of owning an RV. From installing solar panels for off-grid adventures to fixing the occasional wear and tear, these costs sneak up on you.

Understanding the financial landscape of RV ownership and camping isn't just about crunching numbers; it's about preparing yourself for the journey ahead. It's about ensuring that each adventure on the road is met with excitement rather than stress over unforeseen expenses. So, buckle up and get ready to navigate this labyrinth of costs—it's all part of the adventure.

The world of RV ownership and camping expenses resembles a colorful mosaic, where various costs blend to paint the financial picture of your adventures. Let's zoom in and decipher these costs while throwing in some real-world insights to guide you through this terrain.

First on the list is the purchase price, a vast spectrum ranging from $6,000 to $20,000 for a pop-up camper and stretching to several hundred thousand dollars for a luxurious Class A motorhome. Finding the right balance between initial costs and future maintenance expenses is key to aligning with your budget and needs.

Next up: insurance. Depending on your RV type and coverage, expect annual premiums from $300 to $800 for trailers and from $1,000 to $2,000 for motorhomes. Comparing quotes can help you secure the best coverage without breaking the bank.

Routine maintenance is vital. Setting aside $1,000 to $2,000 annually ensures smooth running, but unforeseen repairs can spike costs.

Fuel keeps your wheels turning, averaging 8–10 miles per gallon for Class A motorhomes. Covering 10,000 miles annually at $3 per gallon could set you back $3,000 to $4,000 in fuel expenses.

Campground fees are diverse, ranging from $25 to $50 per night at state parks to over $100 at luxury resorts. Monthly stays might average $500 to $1,000 based on amenities.

Unpredictable repairs can cost 1-2% of your RV's value each year, approximately $500 to $1,000 for a $50,000 RV.

Optional upgrades, such as solar panels or entertainment systems, demand separate budgeting. Solar setups range from $500 to several thousand, while top-notch entertainment systems may exceed $1,500.

Storage fees, towing expenses, utilities, and personal costs are additional financial factors that shouldn't be overlooked.

Understanding these costs goes beyond budgeting—it's about preparedness. Building an emergency fund, shopping around for insurance, and considering long-term expenses when choosing an

RV type is critical. Planning and realistic expectations are your guides through this financial journey.

FINANCING OPTIONS FOR PURCHASING AN RV

Let's unravel the world of financing options for getting your dream RV. We're diving into loans, leases, and more, so you're all set to make the best choice that fits your wallet.

Financing options like loans and leases can make realizing your dream RV purchase possible without breaking the bank. Loans allow you to spread out costs over a set repayment term, usually 5–20 years. They may be secured with the RV as collateral or unsecured based solely on your credit. Loans open doors to better interest rates, help build a credit history and divide payments into manageable bites. But keep an eye on interest rates tied to your credit score and loan amount; higher rates drastically increase total costs. Also, consider the RV's depreciation; if the loan value ends up higher than the RV's resale value, you could face financial loss when selling.

✚ Pros:

- **Spread cost over time:** Loans allow spreading out the RV's cost over an extended period, making it more manageable.
- **Potentially lower rates:** Securing a loan with good credit might result in lower interest rates, reducing the overall cost.
- **Boosts credit:** Consistent, on-time loan payments can positively impact credit scores.

━ Cons:

- **Depreciation risk:** RVs depreciate over time, potentially leaving owners with a loan balance higher than the RV's value.
- **Interest rates based on credit:** Rates might be higher based on creditworthiness, impacting the total loan cost.

Leasing, alternatively, carries lower upfront expenses and fixed monthly payments, like renting. You can conveniently upgrade to a newer model when the term ends. But leases come with mileage restrictions, thorough inspections where excessive wear-and-tear may incur fees, and no RV ownership rights. Beyond loans and leases, explore manufacturer financing incentives that offer discounted rates to push sales. Credit unions may extend special financing offers specifically for their members. Dealers themselves may run periodic promotions with reduced interest rates or favorable terms on certain brands or models.

✚ Pros:

- **Lower upfront costs:** Leasing often requires lower upfront costs than buying, making it more accessible initially.
- **Newer RVs:** Lease terms usually involve newer RVs, offering the latest models and technologies.
- **Switch to a new RV:** At the end of the lease, individuals can switch to a new RV hassle-free.

— Cons:

- **Mileage limits:** Leases usually have mileage limits, and exceeding them can lead to extra fees.
- **Wear and tear charges:** Damages beyond normal wear might incur penalties at the lease end.
- **No ownership:** Leasing means no ownership or equity in the RV at the lease conclusion.

Manufacturer financing, credit unions, and dealer incentives:

✚ Pros:

- **Potential deals and perks:** Manufacturers often provide attractive offers or perks.
- **Favorable rates from credit unions:** Members of credit unions might access more favorable rates.
- **Reduced rates or special terms:** Dealers sometimes offer reduced interest rates or special terms for specific RV models.

— Cons:

- **Limited availability:** Manufacturer financing or dealer incentives might not be as flexible as other options.
- **Eligibility criteria:** Access to manufacturer deals or credit union rates might be subject to specific criteria or membership requirements.

Each financing option has its own unique advantages and drawbacks, making it crucial for individuals to evaluate their financial situation and long-term goals before choosing the most suitable option for purchasing an RV.

Mapping out your financial road trip starts with number crunching—tallying your income, current savings, and monthly expenses like housing, debt payments, transportation, and living costs. This helps determine the payment you can reasonably afford each month for an RV loan or lease. Also, budget for operating costs like fuel, maintenance, storage, insurance fees, and campground rates, which all add up. With your budget foundation set, examine your credit score, which significantly impacts the loan terms lenders will extend. Scores above 700 are ideal for the best rates, while scores below 650 may mean sky-high interest levels or loan denial altogether. Tracking your detailed finances and having excellent credit essentially serve as VIP passes to prime lending conditions when financing your RV escapade adventures ahead!

BUDGETING TIPS FOR CAMPING TRIPS AND LONG-TERM TRAVEL

Embarking on a camping trip or long-term RV travel demands savvy budgeting. Practical tips span from short camping excursions to extended journeys—think cost-effective meal planning and leveraging free camping spots.

Short camping excursions:

1. **Cost-effective meal planning:** Embrace meal-prepping before the trip. Plan simple yet nutritious meals and pack essential cooking utensils to avoid buying expensive campsite meals.
2. **Free camping spots:** Research free or low-cost camping locations. Utilize apps and websites that list free

camping areas, enabling you to save on accommodation fees.

3. **Gear renting or borrowing:** For one-time trips, consider renting or borrowing camping gear instead of purchasing, cutting down on initial expenses.

4. **DIY camping supplies:** Get crafty and create your camping essentials. DIY fire starters, reusable utensils, and even homemade first aid kits can save money in the long run.

5. **Reusable gear:** Invest in reusable camping gear that can be utilized for multiple trips, like durable tents or portable stoves.

Long-term RV travel:

1. **Detailed expense breakdown:** Create a comprehensive budget covering fuel costs, campground fees, groceries, entertainment, and maintenance. Allow flexibility for unexpected expenses.

2. **Work camping and volunteering:** Consider work camping opportunities where you work a few hours in exchange for a campsite, reducing accommodation costs.

3. **Budget-friendly activities:** Engage in low-cost or free activities such as hiking, birdwatching, or visiting national parks that offer annual passes or free entry days.

4. **Flexible travel routes:** Adjust travel plans based on budget considerations. Stay longer in budget-friendly areas or explore regions with varying cost structures.

5. **Maintenance savings:** Regularly maintain your RV to prevent costly repairs down the line. Basic upkeep reduces the risk of unexpected expenses.

Financial planning:

1. **Setting realistic expectations:** Craft a budget that aligns with your lifestyle and travel aspirations. Be realistic about expenses and the level of comfort you desire.

2. **Emergency funds:** Allocate funds for emergencies or unexpected repairs. Having a safety net minimizes the impact of unforeseen expenses.

3. **Review and adjust:** Periodically review your spending against your budget. Adjust categories as needed and assess areas where you can cut back or reallocate funds.

4. **Technology assistance:** Utilize budgeting apps or tools to track expenses in real time. These tools offer insights into spending patterns, aiding in better financial management.

5. **Consistency and discipline:** Stick to your budget by maintaining discipline. Avoid impulse purchases and focus on experiences that truly matter to you.

Effective budgeting ensures that each camping trip or RV adventure is not just affordable but also enjoyable. It offers financial security, allowing you to relish the beauty of the outdoors without worrying about your bank balance.

Of course, you also have the option to rent an RV. But should you rent?

Renting an RV offers flexibility, convenience, and a chance to explore the RV lifestyle without the commitment of ownership. Rental companies typically offer various types of RVs, from compact camper vans to spacious motorhomes. Class A, B, or C motorhomes, travel trailers, pop-up campers, and camper vans are commonly available for rent. Each type caters to different travel preferences, group sizes, and amenities.

Renting an RV offers newcomers a chance to explore various RV types, helping them find the ideal match before making a purchase. Rental companies take care of maintenance and insurance and often offer roadside assistance, lessening the burden on renters.

This flexibility allows tailoring the RV to fit the specific needs of each trip, selecting the right size, amenities, and features. For those who camp infrequently, renting can be more cost-effective than owning and maintaining an RV, eliminating the hefty upfront investment required for purchase.

Additionally, renting enables individuals to experiment with different RV models, sizes, and features without the commitment of ownership. Rental companies handle maintenance and repairs, sparing renters from ongoing costs and the hassles of upkeep.

Moreover, there's no long-term commitment, making it an ideal choice for occasional campers or those uncertain about long-term RV ownership. Rental agreements often include insurance coverage, and renters can bypass the need for long-term storage when the RV is not in use.

Customizing the RV to personal preferences is limited when renting, as modifications are often restricted.

Frequent or extended trips might lead to accumulating rental fees, possibly exceeding the long-term cost of owning an RV.

During peak seasons, RV availability might be limited, and rental agreements typically include mileage restrictions and specific usage guidelines, which can impact flexibility.

There are a few considerations that you need to keep in mind should you decide to rent.

Booking in advance: Especially during peak seasons, booking early secures better rates and ensures availability.

Understanding fees: Rental fees vary based on the type of RV, duration, mileage, and season. Be aware of additional charges for exceeding mileage limits or making late returns.

Insurance coverage: Rental companies offer insurance options, but it's essential to understand the coverage and any additional liabilities.

Inspecting the RV: Before hitting the road, conduct a thorough inspection of the RV, noting any existing damages, to avoid liability issues upon return.

Comparison shopping: Research multiple rental companies, comparing prices, including amenities, insurance coverage, and customer reviews.

Special offers: Look for discounts for extended rentals, off-season bookings, first-time renters, or loyalty programs.

Additional amenities: Some rentals include extras like kitchenware, bedding, and camping gear, potentially saving on packing and buying additional items.

Plan and book early: Reserve well in advance, especially for peak seasons or popular travel periods, to secure better rates.

Read the fine print: Review rental agreements thoroughly, understanding policies on mileage limits, additional fees, insurance coverage, and cancellation policies.

Inspect before renting: Conduct a thorough inspection of the RV before renting, noting any existing damages to avoid liability issues upon return.

Renting an RV offers a taste of the RV lifestyle without a long-term commitment. It's a fantastic option for exploring diverse destinations and experiencing the freedom of the open road without the responsibilities of ownership.

Choosing between renting and owning an RV depends on individual preferences, frequency of use, and budget considerations. Renting is often a favorable option for occasional campers seeking flexibility without long-term commitments or maintenance responsibilities. It's crucial to weigh these factors and consider rental terms before making a decision.

Understanding the financial landscape sets the stage for the next crucial step—choosing the perfect RV or tent. Aligning with your budget and camping style, the next chapter explores this decision-making process, a cornerstone of your outdoor adventures.

CHAPTER 3

CHOOSING THE RIGHT RV OR TENT

With the RV industry offering over a dozen types of RVs and countless tent options, choosing the right one can feel like navigating a maze. However, this decision marks the cornerstone of a camping adventure—getting it right sets the stage for memorable experiences. This chapter isn't just about picking between options; it's about understanding needs, preferences, and functionalities to ensure a perfect camping haven. Here, we unravel the complexities, guiding you through the process to discover the ideal RV or tent that aligns seamlessly with your camping dreams. Whether you're drawn to the convenience of an RV or the simplicity of tent camping, this journey toward your camping haven begins now.

TYPES OF RVS: CLASS A, B, C, AND TRAVEL TRAILERS

So many choices, so little time! I know all you want to do is get on the road, smell the fresh forest air, and leave all your worries behind. However, with the wide range of RVs on the market, choosing one for your adventures can become overwhelming. One of our mottos is "Why not make everything an adventure." This includes choosing the right vehicle for the next camping trip, and to help you on this fun-filled journey, let's dive into the world of RVs and see what they have to offer.

Class A RVs

Class A RVs are the palaces on wheels in the RV world, epitomizing luxury and comfort. These colossal vehicles are mobile mansions, boasting expansive interiors reminiscent of a well-appointed home. Spanning from 25 to a whopping 45 feet in length, these giants offer an abundance of space to indulge in the creature comforts of life on the road.

Class A RVs are synonymous with space. With their generous square footage, they accommodate luxurious amenities such as full-sized kitchens with modern appliances, bathrooms with ample facilities, multiple private bedrooms, and lavish entertainment systems. Some models even include slide-outs that expand living areas at the touch of a button.

Due to their comfort and spaciousness, Class A RVs are ideal for extended road trips or as full-time residences. Their luxurious interiors cater to individuals or families seeking the utmost comfort while on the move. These vehicles offer a true home-away-from-home experience, making them suitable for those embracing the RV lifestyle as their primary residence.

Pros and cons of Class A RVs:

✚ Pros

- **Luxurious amenities:** These RVs are decked out with high-end amenities akin to upscale homes, ensuring a comfortable and enjoyable experience on the road.
- **Ideal for long trips or full-time living:** Their spaciousness and comforts make them perfect for extended journeys or as a permanent residence.
- **Wide variety of floor plans:** Class A RVs offer a diverse range of floor plans and customization options, allowing buyers to tailor the vehicle to their preferences.

▬ Cons

- **Lower fuel efficiency:** Due to their size and weight, Class A RVs tend to have lower fuel efficiency compared to smaller models.
- **Challenging maneuverability:** Their size can make maneuvering in tight spaces, such as navigating through crowded cities or fitting into smaller campsites, a bit challenging.

Class A RVs are the epitome of luxury and comfort on the road, providing an extravagant traveling experience but requiring a bit more finesse when it comes to handling and fuel consumption.

Class B RVs (Campervans)

Class B RVs, colloquially known as campervans, are the nimble nomads of the RV world. Compact and resembling oversized vans, these vehicles offer a pared-down yet functional living space, ideal for solo adventurers or couples seeking simplicity without compromising on convenience.

Measuring between 16 and 22 feet in length, Class B RVs maximize every inch of space. Despite their compact size, they manage to house the basic amenities essential for life on the road. Inside, you'll find sleeping quarters, a petite kitchenette, and occasionally a compact bathroom—providing the essentials for comfortable travel without excess frills.

Campervans excel in their ease of maneuverability and driving. Their smaller size allows for nimble navigation through city streets, tight campsites, or winding scenic roads. Moreover, their more modest dimensions contribute to better fuel efficiency compared to larger, bulkier RV models.

Pros and cons of Class B RVs:

+ Pros

- **Better fuel efficiency:** Due to their smaller size and lighter weight, Class B RVs tend to offer superior fuel efficiency, making them more economical on longer journeys.
- **Ease of driving and maneuverability:** Their compact design and van-like structure make them effortless to drive and park, offering versatility in urban environments and nature exploration.
- **Versatile for city and nature exploration:** Their maneuverability makes them equally suitable for urban escapades and off-the-grid adventures.

━ Cons

- **Limited space and amenities:** While they provide the basics, Class B RVs have restricted space and amenities compared to larger models, which might feel restrictive during extended trips or for larger groups.

Class B RVs, the campervans, shine in their maneuverability and simplicity, offering a convenient and efficient mode of travel for individuals or couples seeking a cozy and manageable home on wheels.

Class C RVs

Class C RVs strike a balanced middle ground between the expansive Class A models and the compact Class Bs. They're recognized by their truck or van chassis, often seen with an extended cab-over section—a distinguishing feature that maximizes interior space while offering a more manageable driving experience.

Ranging between 20 and 33 feet in length, Class C RVs provide a comfortable living space without the grandiosity of Class A models. They're spacious enough to accommodate sleeping quarters, a kitchen, a bathroom, and several amenities suited for small families or groups of travelers.

Ideal for families or groups seeking comfort without the challenges of handling a larger RV, Class C models strike a chord between spaciousness and ease of driving. The cab-over design often houses additional sleeping or storage space, making efficient use of the available area.

Pros and cons of Class C RVs:

+ Pros

- **Comfortable amenities for small groups:** With a thoughtful layout, Class C RVs offer ample space and amenities suitable for small families or groups, providing a comfortable traveling experience.
- **Easier to drive than Class A models:** Their manageable size and familiar truck or van chassis make them more approachable and easier to handle compared to their larger counterparts.
- **Balanced space and maneuverability:** Offering a good balance between living space and maneuverability, Class C RVs provide enough room without overwhelming size.

— Cons

- **Moderate fuel efficiency:** While not as fuel-efficient as smaller Class B models, Class C RVs offer moderate fuel efficiency considering their size and amenities.
- **Limited living space compared to Class A models:** Despite their comfort, they don't match the spaciousness of Class A models, which might be a drawback for those seeking more expansive living quarters.

Class C RVs strike a chord for travelers seeking a comfortable, spacious, yet manageable RV experience, making them an appealing choice for small families or groups looking to balance comfort with ease of driving.

Travel Trailers

Travel trailers are like mobile homes, but the twist is that you'll need a separate vehicle to tow them along. They come in a range of sizes, stretching from 12 to 35 feet, offering diverse layouts and amenities to suit varied needs.

Travel trailers are quite the chameleons, offering different sizes and layouts to cater to various preferences. Whether you're after a cozy couple's retreat or a family-friendly space, these trailers have a plan for everyone.

The beauty of these trailers lies in their detachability. Once you arrive at your destination, you can unhitch the trailer, leaving your towing vehicle free for sightseeing and exploration. It's like having the best of both worlds—a cozy nest and a set of wheels for adventures.

Pros and cons of travel trailers:

✚ Pros

- **Diverse sizes and layouts:** From compact models to more spacious options, travel trailers offer a wide array of sizes and floor plans to match different preferences.
- **Detachable convenience:** The ability to detach the trailer at your destination provides flexibility—your towing vehicle becomes a standalone explorer, freeing you up for local adventures.

- **Generally more affordable:** Compared to motorized RVs, travel trailers often come with a more budget-friendly price tag, making them accessible to a broader range of travelers.

━ Cons

- **Requires a tow vehicle:** You'll need a separate vehicle, like a truck or an SUV, capable of towing the trailer, adding an extra element to consider for travel.
- **Setup and leveling:** Setting up and leveling the trailer at your campsite can take some time and effort, which might not appeal to those seeking a quicker setup process.

Travel trailers are a versatile choice for those who want to bring the comforts of home on their travels. They offer diverse options, allowing for exploration and customization, albeit with the need for a tow vehicle and a bit of patience during setup.

Key Features to Look For

Keep the following considerations in mind when choosing the perfect getaway vehicle for you and your family:

1. **Space and comfort:** Think about the crew you're rolling with and their comfort preferences. Check for sufficient sleeping quarters, ample storage for gear and supplies, and a living area that suits your desired comfort level. Ensure everyone has their cozy spot, especially during those long hauls or extended stays.

2. **Build quality and amenities:** Quality matters! Assess the construction quality of the RV—durability, insulation for all seasons, and the overall reliability of the appliances. Dive into the amenities, too. Does it sport a well-equipped kitchen for your culinary escapades? What about the bathroom setup? Entertainment options? Also, look into slide-out features that can add more space when parked.

3. **Budget considerations:** Stay true to your budget! Identify the must-have features for your comfort and prioritize them within your overall financial plan. It's a balancing act—ensuring comfort without breaking the bank. Don't sway too much from your budgetary boundaries while on this quest for the ideal RV.

4. **User reviews and expert opinions:** Time for some detective work! Before sealing the deal, delve into user reviews and tap into expert opinions. Real-life experiences shared by other RVers can be gold. They often shed light on the practicality, functionality, and real-world performance of specific RV models. These insights can make or break your decision.

The right RV isn't just about aesthetics; it's about functionality and comfort on the open road. So, go forth armed with these considerations, and you'll be cruising in your ideal RV in no time!

CHOOSING THE RIGHT TENT FOR YOUR NEEDS

Choosing a tent can be quite an adventure in itself. I remember the excitement and the dizzying array of options when I first set out to buy my very first tent. It's a bit like stepping into a whole new world, surrounded by different shapes, sizes, materials, and features. You've got everything from compact one-person tents that snugly fit into a backpack to sprawling family tents that practically have a zip code of their own. The options almost seem endless.

It's not just about picking a tent; it's about finding one that suits your needs, your camping style, and the kind of adventures you're planning. You've got dome tents, cabin tents, teepee tents, and even tunnel tents. Each with its own perks, quirks, and even a difficulty level for setting up. Some are light as a feather, perfect for trekking miles on the trail, while others are sturdy enough to withstand unpredictable weather conditions.

Oh, and don't get me started on the features! From built-in vestibules for storing gear to ventilation systems that rival high-tech gadgets, tents these days come with bells and whistles that can make your head spin. Plus, don't forget about the waterproofing, the seams, and the poles; there's a lot to consider to ensuring a cozy night's sleep, rain or shine.

Choosing the right tent isn't about finding a shelter; it's about finding your home away from home, your sanctuary in the wilderness. It's about comfort, protection, and that feeling of security as you drift off to sleep cocooned under the stars.

Dome Tents

Dome tents are renowned for their versatile design and structural stability, making them a popular choice among campers. Characterized by their arched structure, these tents are formed with flexible poles that cross over the tent's center. This design creates a dome-like shape, contributing to their stability.

Their construction typically involves a simple setup process due to the fewer number of poles and the crossover design, making them quick to pitch. Dome tents excel in various camping conditions, from wilderness adventures to festival camping. Their adaptability makes them suitable for different terrains and weather conditions.

The aerodynamic shape minimizes flat surfaces, reducing vulnerability to strong winds. This stability in windy conditions makes dome tents a reliable choice for breezy locations.

Pros and cons of dome tents:

+ Pros

- **Stability in the wind:** Their sturdy structure and rounded design offer excellent stability, ensuring the tent remains robust even in gusty winds.
- **Quick assembly:** The simplicity of their setup means these tents can be pitched swiftly, making them

convenient for shorter stays or when you need to set up camp quickly.

- **Headroom at the center:** While the sidewalls slope, the dome's peak often provides sufficient headspace, especially in larger models.

— Cons

- **Less standing room:** The curved walls, while contributing to stability, can limit the amount of vertical space at the tent's edges. This might reduce standing room near the tent's sides.

Dome tents strike a balance between stability, versatility, and ease of setup, making them a favored option for campers seeking reliable shelter across various camping scenarios. Their lightweight nature and wind-resilient structure make them a go-to choice.

Cabin Tents

Cabin tents are renowned for their spacious design, offering campers a home-like feel amidst the great outdoors. Cabin tents are identifiable by their vertical walls that maximize interior space, allowing you to stand comfortably throughout most of the tent's area. Many cabin-style tents feature dividers or multiple compartments, creating separate spaces within the tent, resembling rooms in a house.

Cabin tents are well-suited for family camping trips, providing ample space to accommodate several campers. Their roomy design offers comfort for families, including children or pets. They are ideal for extended stays at campsites where comfort and space matter. The spacious interior allows for more relaxed living and the storage of camping gear.

Pros and cons of cabin tents:

+ Pros

- **Ample headroom:** The vertical walls create a generous ceiling height throughout the tent, maximizing standing space. This design allows you to move around comfortably without having to crouch.
- **Spacious interior:** With their roomy design, cabin tents offer plenty of living space, making them an excellent choice for families or groups.

- **Comfort for extended stays:** The multiple rooms or compartments allow for a more organized living space, providing privacy and separation for different activities.

— Cons

- **Bulkier and heavier:** Due to their design and larger size, cabin tents tend to be bulkier and heavier than other tent types. This may pose challenges during transportation and can require more effort to set up.
- **Complex setup:** The added features like dividers or multiple rooms might make cabin tents slightly more complex to set up compared to simpler tent designs.

Cabin tents prioritize comfort and spaciousness, making them an excellent choice for those seeking a tent that resembles a mini-home while camping. Despite their bulkier size and potentially more involved setup, their roomy interiors and versatility often make them the preferred choice for your family-oriented camping trips or longer stays at campgrounds.

Backpacking Tents

Backpacking tents are specifically crafted to cater to the needs of hikers and outdoor enthusiasts looking for lightweight and portable shelters. These tents are meticulously designed using lightweight materials to ensure they're easily portable during hiking or backpacking trips. Backpacking tents prioritize packability, folding down into a compact size to fit conveniently into a backpack.

These tents are well-suited for solo hikers or small groups embarking on outdoor adventures where weight and packability are essential considerations. Their lightweight and compact design makes them ideal for hikers and trekkers who cover substantial distances on foot and need a portable shelter.

Pros and cons of backpacking tents:

+ Pros

- **Lightweight and portable:** Their primary advantage lies in their lightweight construction, ensuring they're easy to carry, making them a favorite among backpackers and hikers.
- **Compact and packable:** Backpacking tents are designed to minimize size when packed, ensuring they fit snugly into a backpack without adding excess weight.

— Cons

- **Limited space:** Due to their emphasis on being lightweight and compact, backpacking tents offer limited interior space, compromising on roominess.
- **Less comfort for extended stays:** Their compact design can result in less comfort for longer stays, as they may lack the spaciousness and amenities found in larger tents.

Backpacking tents are a go-to choice for adventurers seeking shelter that won't weigh them down during their outdoor expeditions. While they excel in portability and weight-saving features, they may sacrifice some comfort and living space in exchange for their lightweight and compact design, making them better suited for shorter stays or trips that prioritize mobility and efficiency.

Tunnel Tents

Tunnel tents are a popular choice among campers, particularly families, seeking spacious and well-structured shelter. Characterized by their elongated, tunnel-like structure, created by arched flexible poles that run lengthwise, offering a spacious interior. Often designed with separate compartments for sleeping and living, providing families or larger groups with designated spaces.

Tunnel tents are an excellent option for your large family camping trips, offering a generous amount of space that's divided into separate areas for added privacy and comfort. Ideal when you want to prioritize roominess and prefer having distinct living, dining, and sleeping spaces within the tent.

Pros and cons of tunnel tents:

+ Pros

- **Roominess:** One of the primary advantages is the spaciousness they offer, making them comfortable for families or groups needing ample interior space.
- **Good headroom:** The arched structure typically provides decent headroom throughout the tent's length, allowing occupants to move around comfortably.
- **Wind resistance:** Their elongated shape and sturdy pole structure often contribute to excellent wind resistance, making them suitable for varying weather conditions.

— Cons

- **Setup time:** Due to their design with multiple poles, tunnel tents may take a bit longer to set up compared to simpler tent types.

- **Bulkier design:** While spacious, the pole structure and size can make them bulkier and more cumbersome to transport compared to smaller, more compact tents.

Tunnel tents are a fantastic option for those seeking a roomy and well-structured camping shelter, particularly families or groups who appreciate separate living areas within the tent. Their spacious design, offering separate compartments and good wind resistance, makes them well-suited for extended camping trips where comfort and ample space are essential. However, their setup may take a bit more time due to the complex pole structure.

Geodesic Tents

Geodesic tents are robust and well-suited for demanding outdoor environments. Geodesic tents feature a dome-shaped structure with numerous intersecting poles, creating a complex yet highly stable framework. They're designed with crisscrossing poles that intersect to form triangles, adding strength and stability to the tent's overall structure.

These tents are best suited for challenging weather conditions, making them ideal for expeditions, mountaineering, or any scenario where extreme durability and stability are essential. Geodesic tents excel in extreme environments, providing reliable shelter against strong winds, heavy snow loads, and harsh weather.

Pros and cons of geodesic tents:

✚ Pros

- **Exceptional stability:** The interconnected pole structure offers unparalleled stability, making these tents reliable and sturdy even in adverse weather conditions.
- **Durability:** Built to withstand harsh elements, geodesic tents are durable and can endure rough usage during demanding outdoor activities.

— Cons

- **Heavier build:** The robust construction and multiple poles often result in a heavier tent, which might be less suitable for lightweight or casual camping where portability is a priority.
- **Complex setup:** Due to their intricate pole configuration, setting up a geodesic tent can be more involved and may require some familiarity with its assembly.

Geodesic tents shine in extreme conditions, providing exceptional stability and resilience against harsh weather, making them a top choice for adventurers, mountaineers, or anyone facing rugged outdoor settings. Their reliable structure and durability come at the cost of being slightly heavier and requiring a more complex setup, but for those needing uncompromising stability in challenging environments, the trade-off is often well worth it.

Teepee Tents

Teepee tents offer a unique camping experience with their distinctive design and features. They are characterized by their conical or pyramid-like shape, often supported by a single central pole. Teepee tents typically provide ample space inside due to their design, offering sufficient room for occupants.

Teepees are ideal for accommodating multiple occupants, making them suitable for group camping or family trips. Teepee tents often boast a straightforward setup process, allowing for quick assembly compared to more complex tent structures. Their versatility makes them suitable for various camping styles, from casual outings to festivals and traditional camping experiences.

Pros and cons of teepee tents:

✚ Pros

- **Roominess:** Their conical shape provides ample floor space, allowing occupants to move freely within the tent.
- **Simple setup:** Teepee tents are known for their relatively easy setup, often requiring only one central pole for support.
- **Good ventilation:** The design often includes openings or vents at the top, aiding in airflow and ensuring decent ventilation inside the tent.

▬ Cons:

- **Weather vulnerability:** In extreme weather conditions, teepee tents might lack the stability and structural integrity of more robust tents, making them less suitable for harsh environments.
- **Limited headroom:** While offering plenty of floor space, teepee tents may have limited headroom toward the tent's edges due to their sloping walls.

Teepee tents are an excellent choice for group camping trips or those seeking a straightforward setup process without compromising too much on space. However, their design may render them less stable in extreme weather conditions, and the sloping walls can limit headroom toward the edges. Despite these limitations, teepee tents remain a popular option for various camping experiences due to their spacious interiors and easy assembly.

Pop-Up Tents

Pop-up tents are renowned for their rapid assembly and convenient design, offering an easy camping solution for various outings. These tents feature collapsible frames or spring-loaded mechanisms, allowing them to pop up into shape instantly. Designed for portability, they often fold down into a compact shape for easy transportation and storage. They're primarily intended for accommodating smaller camping groups or individual campers.

Perfect for spontaneous weekend getaways or short camping trips where ease and speed of setup are crucial, pop-up tents are popular among festival-goers due to their quick assembly and portability, offering a hassle-free shelter solution.

Pros and cons of pop-up tents:

+ Pros

- **Ultra-quick setup:** The standout feature is their rapid setup, often requiring minimal effort or manual assembly.
- **Convenient portability:** Designed to be lightweight and easily portable, they're ideal for campers seeking hassle-free transportation.
- **Convenience:** Ideal for those seeking a no-fuss camping experience, especially when convenience takes precedence over spaciousness.

— Cons

- **Space limitations:** Typically, pop-up tents offer limited space, making them more suitable for smaller groups or solo campers.
- **Wind stability:** Due to their instant setup design, pop-up tents might be less sturdy in windy conditions compared to more robust tent structures.

Pop-up tents shine in scenarios where convenience and quick assembly are top priorities. While they offer rapid setup and convenient portability, their space may be limited, making them more suitable for smaller groups or solo campers. Additionally, in windy conditions, their instant setup design might render them less stable compared to sturdier tent options. Despite these limitations, pop-up tents remain a popular choice for campers seeking quick and effortless shelter solutions.

Each type of tent offers unique features tailored to different camping needs. Understanding their characteristics helps in choosing the most suitable tent for a specific camping trip or outdoor adventure.

Choosing the right RV or tent is merely the opening act. The subsequent chapter delves into the art of setting up effectively. It's a crucial step in transforming your chosen haven into a cozy, functional space amidst the wilderness. A well-chosen RV or tent sets the stage for an unforgettable camping escapade.

CHAPTER 4

SETTING UP YOUR CAMPSITE

Did you know that a well-arranged campsite can be the unsung hero of your outdoor adventure, influencing everything from your sleep quality to your overall safety? The right setup can turn a good trip into an unforgettable one. That's why mastering the art of campsite arrangement is a game-changer for any camper, and in this chapter, I'll walk you through the essential steps to become a pro at setting up your perfect camping haven.

STEP-BY-STEP GUIDE TO SETTING UP AN RV OR TENT

Setting up camp is the cornerstone of any camping adventure, whether it's in the cozy confines of an RV or the snug embrace of a tent. Knowing the ins and outs of how to set up your campsite can transform a mere patch of land into your home away from home. In this comprehensive guide, we'll walk through the step-by-step process for setting up both an RV and a tent, ensuring a smooth and enjoyable camping experience from the moment you arrive at your chosen site.

Setting up an RV

By following these steps, you can set up your RV efficiently, creating a comfortable living space to enjoy your camping experience to the fullest.

Positioning and Leveling

Look for a flat and level area to park your RV. This not only enhances comfort while resting inside but also aids in the proper functioning of appliances like refrigerators, stoves, and heaters. Parking on uneven terrain can cause appliances to work improperly and could even damage them.

On uneven ground, leveling blocks become your best friend. These blocks go under the RV's tires to create a stable, level surface. They're essential for preventing the RV from tilting, which not only affects comfort but also impacts the functionality of internal systems like refrigerators, making them less efficient.

Once your RV is parked on the leveled surface, extend the stabilizing jacks. These jacks are typically located on the corners of the RV. Extending them not only reduces the rocking motion inside the RV but also significantly enhances stability. This creates a secure foundation, especially when you're moving around inside the vehicle. It's crucial for safety and a more comfortable experience, especially if you have multiple people moving around or if you're parked in a windy area.

Electrical and Water Hookup

If a power pedestal is available at the campsite, use a power cord suitable for your RV to connect to the power source. Ensure the breakers on the pedestal are turned off before plugging in. Alternatively, if no power source is available, set up a generator that matches your RV's electrical needs. Generators provide electricity when camping off-grid but ensure they're placed a safe distance away from the RV to prevent carbon monoxide buildup.

Use a potable water hose to link the campsite's water supply to your RV's water inlet. Make sure the hose fits snugly without leaks. Turn on the water supply gradually to avoid sudden pressure surges. Use a water pressure regulator to protect your RV's plumbing system from high water pressure, especially when using external sources.

Connect one end of the sewer hose to the RV's waste outlet and the other end to the dump station or sewer hookup at the campsite. Ensure a tight and secure connection to prevent leaks or spills. For hygienic disposal, always dump black water (from toilets) before gray water (from sinks and showers).

Open the black water tank valve first to empty the contents into the sewer. Once emptied, close the black water valve, and then open the gray water valve to flush out the hose with cleaner water. Always follow the campground's guidelines and regulations regarding waste disposal.

Properly setting up these utilities ensures a convenient and comfortable camping experience while maintaining respect for the environment and the campground's regulations. Regular maintenance and care of these connections are essential for long-term functionality and to prevent any issues during your stay.

Awning and Outdoor Setup

Unfold the awning gently, ensuring there are no obstructions like tree branches or cables above. Most awnings have simple mechanisms for extension; follow the manufacturer's instructions carefully. Some may have automated or manual cranks to extend and retract.

Use the stabilizing rods or legs provided with the awning to secure it firmly to the ground. Anchor the legs or rods using stakes or weights, especially in windy conditions, to prevent them from lifting or swaying.

Set up chairs, tables, and outdoor equipment strategically to create a comfortable and inviting outdoor space. Ensure furniture is on stable ground and properly positioned for relaxation, meals, or other activities.

Add outdoor rugs or mats to define the area and keep dirt at bay. Use lighting such as string lights or lanterns for evening ambiance and better visibility. Consider sunshades or screens to shield from excessive sunlight or insects.

Always secure loose items during windy conditions to prevent damage or accidents. Be mindful of the weight distribution on the awning and avoid hanging heavy objects that might cause imbalance or strain on the structure.

Proper setup and arrangement of your outdoor area not only create a comfortable living space but also contribute significantly to an enjoyable camping experience. Always follow manufacturer instructions for awning setup and consider the weather conditions when arranging outdoor furniture for safety and comfort.

Interior Arrangements

If your RV is equipped with slide-outs, deploy them carefully once you're parked and leveled. Ensure the area around the slide-outs is clear to avoid any obstructions. Once extended, slide-outs significantly increase interior space, providing more room to move around, lounge, or set up additional furniture.

Check the functionality of all appliances, like the stove, refrigerator, microwave, and any other equipment available in your RV. Ensure they are operational and in good working condition before relying on them during your stay.

Test the lighting fixtures, HVAC system, water heater, and plumbing utilities to make sure everything is functioning correctly. This step is crucial for ensuring a comfortable and hassle-free stay.

Keep in mind any safety instructions provided by the manufacturer regarding the use of appliances and utilities. Be cautious with gas-operated appliances and make sure they are properly ventilated.

Taking the time to extend slide-outs for added space and checking the functionality of appliances and utilities enhances the overall comfort and functionality of your RV stay, making it a more enjoy-able experience.

Setting up a Tent

Following these steps will help you set up your tent efficiently, creating a safe and comfortable camping experience amidst nature's elements.

1. **Choosing the campsite:** Opt for a level, well-drained area free from rocks and debris; this will offer a comfortable and safe ground for pitching the tent. Orient the tent door away from the prevailing wind direction to reduce exposure and potential discomfort.

2. **Ground cover and tent pitching:** Lay a tarp or groundsheet beneath the tent to shield its bottom from moisture, enhancing durability and protection. Assemble tent poles following the manufacturer's instructions, securing them to establish the tent's structure. Utilize stakes to firmly anchor the tent to the ground, ensuring stability even in windy conditions.

3. **Interior setup:** Arrange sleeping pads, air mattresses, or sleeping bags inside the tent for a comfortable rest. Organize gear and personal items within the tent to optimize space and accessibility. Install lanterns or other lighting sources to ensure adequate illumination during the night.

4. **Weather preparations:** Install the rain fly if your tent has one to protect against rain and ensure a dry interior. Open windows or vents for proper airflow,

adapting to weather conditions for a comfortable atmosphere.

5. **Campsite maintenance:** Maintain a tidy campsite by appropriately disposing of trash and food waste to minimize environmental impact. If using a campfire, ensure it's contained and safely extinguished before departing, preventing potential hazards.

HOW TO SELECT THE PERFECT CAMPSITE

Selecting the ultimate campsite isn't just about finding a spot—it's about uncovering your own personal oasis in the wilderness. Here's your secret map to discovering that perfect camping nook.

Level Ground

Finding level ground is like securing the foundation for a good night's sleep. Imagine setting up your sleeping bag and then realizing you're on a slope—the next thing you know, you're waking up in the corner of your tent! Avoid this midnight adventure by scouting a spot as flat as you can find. It keeps your sleeping setup cozy and prevents any unwanted rolls.

Also, speaking of soggy surprises, low areas can turn into impromptu ponds after a downpour. That's definitely not the experience you're aiming for! So steer clear of these low spots to dodge any unintentional swimming sessions inside your tent. Opt for higher ground or areas with good drainage to keep your camping spot dry and your adventure free from unexpected water features.

Facility Check

Convenience is king when it comes to choosing your camping spot! Being close to key facilities like restrooms, water sources, and waste disposal spots can make your outdoor experience a whole lot smoother.

Imagine needing the restroom in the middle of the night—it's like a treasure hunt in the dark! That's why camping closer to the facilities, especially restrooms, can be a game-changer, saving you from wandering in the dark or doing a sprint across the campground.

Having easy access to water sources is also a plus. Whether it's for drinking, cooking, or cleaning, it means less hassle and more time enjoying your adventure. And let's not forget waste disposal! Being close to trash bins or designated disposal areas ensures you can easily keep your campsite clean without having to trek far with bags of trash.

So, remember, the closer these facilities are to your campsite, the smoother your camping experience can be, especially during those midnight emergencies!

Shade and Shelter

Shade can be a real game-changer in the great outdoors. When the sun's beating down, finding a spot sheltered by trees or even a natural rock formation can feel like discovering a hidden oasis. It's like stumbling upon a cool, comfortable sanctuary amidst the heat.

And let's talk rain—the unexpected downpour can really dampen the camping mood. Finding a spot with natural shelter, like under a dense tree canopy or behind a rock formation, can be your secret weapon. It's like finding your own cozy nook during a hide-and-seek game, keeping you dry and snug while the rain pours down.

Remember, whether it's for relief from the scorching sun or seeking refuge from raindrops, a camping spot with natural shade or shelter is a real treasure!

Privacy Please

Privacy can be a real luxury in the camping world! If you're not keen on being in the camping hubbub, a quieter spot might just be your ticket to tranquility. It's like stumbling upon your own tucked-away sanctuary amidst the hustle and bustle of the campground.

That little bit of extra distance from the center of activity can feel like discovering your own private slice of camping paradise. Whether it's for a peaceful night's sleep or just some quiet down-time, finding a spot away from the buzz can be a real game-changer.

In the end, finding that perfect camping spot is all about those small but crucial details. Keeping these factors in mind ensures you'll be lounging in your camping haven in no time, enjoying the serenity and relaxation you sought.

Different Environments

Venturing into diverse camping environments brings a spectrum of experiences, each with its own charm and challenges. Understanding the unique landscape of each setting is crucial for a safe and unforgettable outdoor adventure.

Forest Fun

Enjoy the forest by scouting those flat spots under the tree canopy —they provide natural shade and a serene atmosphere. However, watch out for precarious branches or old trees that might pose risks.

Beach Bumming

When beachside, steer clear of areas prone to high tides—unless impromptu ocean swims are on your agenda! Seek out spots sheltered from strong coastal winds for a more relaxed stay.

Mountain Escapades

In mountainous regions, choose camp areas away from low valleys where cold air accumulates. Mind your footing; loose rocks or unexpected slides can quickly change the tone of your mountain escapade.

Nail these tips, and you're on your way to scoring the primo campsite no matter where your adventures take you. Stay safe, and let's keep those campgrounds awesome for everyone!

All About Safety

While adventure often beckons, comfort and safety go hand in hand. Stick to activities within your skill and comfort level. No need to rush; enjoy the journey and gradually explore more challenging adventures as you grow in experience.

Campfire Safety

The flickering glow of a campfire is magical, but safety is priority number one. Adhere to campground regulations—maintain a safe distance from tents and trees, extinguish the fire entirely before calling it a night, and confine flames to designated fire pits. A fire extinguisher within reach adds an extra layer of security against unexpected fire behavior.

Wildlife Etiquette

Nature's friends, like squirrels and raccoons, can get a bit too friendly if they catch a whiff of snacks. Keep edibles securely stored to prevent unplanned critter parties. Show respect for wildlife by keeping a safe distance, refraining from feeding them, and ensuring your trash is properly disposed of to prevent unwanted furry visitors.

Weather Watch

Nature's mood swings can be unpredictable, so it's wise to peek at the forecast before embarking on your adventure. Pack considering potential weather changes—having a well-stocked first aid kit and emergency gear handy is like having a camping superhero by your side.

Campsite Scouting

Take a leisurely walk around your chosen site to spot potential trip hazards. Uneven ground or hidden obstacles might spell trouble, so being aware of these hazards helps prevent unwanted spills.

First Aid Refresher

A quick refresher on basic first aid can be a game-changer in unexpected situations. Basic knowledge, like treating minor cuts or dealing with insect bites, can make a huge difference.

CAMPGROUND ETIQUETTE

Maintaining good campground etiquette is key to enjoying the great outdoors while respecting both nature and your fellow campers.

When the sun sets, tranquility settles in—respect the tranquility during those designated quiet hours. While your tunes might be awesome, not everyone's ready for a spontaneous concert right by their tent!

Pack it in, pack it out—leave no trace behind. Keep the campsite spotless by properly disposing of your trash in designated areas. Leaving the area cleaner than you found it is like spreading good camping vibes!

Just like you value your personal bubble, others cherish their camping sanctuaries too. Respect their privacy by being mindful of their space, and if you're camping with pets, ensure they're considerate of other campers' areas, especially when nature calls.

It's more than a catchy phrase—it's a commitment to preserving nature's beauty. Plan ahead, tread lightly, and leave natural wonders untouched for others to relish. It's like passing on the torch of outdoor appreciation to fellow adventurers!

By embracing these campground etiquette pointers, you're not just ensuring an enjoyable experience for yourself, but you're also leaving the wilderness in its most pristine form for the next batch of outdoor enthusiasts!

With the campsite set up, the next frontier is managing RV hookups and utilities—a crucial aspect of RV camping. The upcoming chapter serves as a guide to navigating these critical elements, ensuring a seamless and enjoyable RV camping experience.

SPREADING THE FREEDOM OF CAMPING

"The camp is the space that is opened when the state of exception begins to become the rule."

GIORGIO AGAMBEN

RVing and camping are routes to a life of freedom. No matter how hectic and stressful your everyday schedule is, the ability to take off for a weekend and set your roots down in nature is an immediate antidote.

That freedom should be accessible to all of us. Camping makes vacationing affordable ... and it makes it possible to turn an average weekend into a mini-vacation. It's not that it isn't accessible. It's simply that it's daunting to the uninitiated.

Perhaps you can relate to that. Perhaps the scenes of puzzles of poles and ropes that I painted in the introduction are all too familiar. If that's the case, I hope you're already feeling better equipped and ready to set yourself up for a camping freedom lifestyle.

Now that we're this far through our journey together, I'd like to ask for your help in reaching more people who have been put off camping and RVing in the past and are looking for a straightforward route to the freedom it offers.

The good news is that it won't take you more than a few minutes.

By leaving a review of this book on Amazon, you'll show other would-be adventurers exactly where they can find all the help they need to get started with RVing and camping.

People are searching for this information, and your review will make it easy for them to find it. It's like building their tent for them ... and who doesn't want that kind of help?!

Thank you so much for your support. Camping offers a level of freedom that we all need. Thank you for helping me bring it to more people.

CHAPTER 5

RV HOOKUPS AND UTILITIES

Becoming a pro at RV hookups and utilities is the unsung hero that makes camping a breeze. This chapter is your gateway to unraveling the secrets of electricity, water, and sewage systems, taking you from a beginner to a savvy RVer in a flash.

Here, we'll break down the intricate universe of RV hookups and utilities, ensuring you're not left stranded—neither in the literal nor metaphorical dark! This chapter dives deep into hands-on guidance and troubleshooting hacks, arming you with the expertise to handle and maximize the potential of these crucial systems.

ELECTRICITY, WATER, AND SEWAGE HOOKUPS

Linking an RV to electricity is about grasping different power levels and adapters. Begin by recognizing the power source at the campground, usually available in 20, 30, or 50-amp electrical connections. Smaller RVs often use a 30-amp connection, whereas larger ones demand a 50-amp connection for their higher power

demands. Adapters serve to convert between various amp connections, guaranteeing that your RV aligns with the campground's
power source.

Power Connections

When connecting, turn off all appliances and the main breaker in
your RV to avoid power surges. Plug in the power cord, ensuring a
snug fit, and use any necessary adapters. Once connected, switch
on the breaker in your RV and then gradually turn on individual
appliances.

To ensure a safe and seamless connection of your RV to the campground's electrical supply, consider these safety measures and
precautions.

Weatherproof outlet covers serve as protective shields for electrical connections in outdoor environments. When connecting
your RV to the campground's electrical supply, these covers are
crucial for safeguarding against weather elements such as rain and
moisture. They are designed to encase the outlet, ensuring a
secure seal that prevents water from seeping into the electrical
connection.

The covers are typically made from durable materials that can
withstand varying weather conditions. They feature a secure
closure mechanism, often with a gasket or seal, to create a barrier
that shields the connection points from moisture infiltration. This
prevents potential electrical hazards, such as short circuits or electrical shocks, which can occur when water comes into contact with
exposed connections.

Using weatherproof outlet covers provides an added layer of safety
and ensures the integrity of your RV's electrical system, allowing

for a secure and reliable power connection even in adverse weather conditions.

Surge protectors and voltage regulators are essential devices for safeguarding your RV's electrical systems from power spikes. These unexpected surges in voltage can potentially damage sensitive electronics and appliances within your RV. Surge protectors are specifically designed to divert excessive voltage away from connected devices, thereby shielding them from potential damage.

Voltage spikes can occur due to various reasons, such as lightning strikes, power grid fluctuations, or even malfunctions in the campground's electrical supply. When these spikes happen, the excess voltage can overwhelm and harm your RV's electrical components.

Surge protectors work by detecting excessive voltage and diverting it away from your RV's electrical system. They act as a barrier, absorbing or redirecting the surge to prevent it from reaching and damaging your RV's appliances, electronics, and internal wiring.

Similarly, voltage regulators help maintain a stable voltage supply to your RV's electrical systems, ensuring that fluctuations or irregularities in the campground's power source do not harm your devices.

Investing in surge protectors or voltage regulators adds a layer of defense against unexpected power surges, providing peace of mind and potentially saving your RV's electronics from costly damage.

Regular inspections of your RV's power cord are crucial to ensuring its safety and reliability. Over time, wear and tear can occur due to exposure to weather elements, constant use, or aging. Periodically examining the power cord helps identify any signs of damage or deterioration, allowing for timely replacements and preventing potential safety hazards.

Here's what to look for during these inspections:

- **Visible wear:** Check the entire length of the power cord for fraying, cuts, or abrasions on the outer insulation. These signs can expose the internal wiring, posing a significant safety risk.
- **Bent or damaged prongs:** Inspect the plug's prongs for bending, cracking, or any damage that might affect their connection to the power source.
- **Loose connections:** Ensure that the cord securely connects to the RV and the power source without any loose or exposed wires.
- **Corrosion or rust:** Examine connectors for any signs of corrosion or rust, especially if the cord has been exposed to moisture.

If you notice any signs of wear, damage, or deterioration during these inspections, it's essential to replace the power cord promptly. Operating an RV with a damaged power cord can lead to electrical malfunctions, pose safety risks, and potentially cause damage to your RV's electrical system or connected appliances. Always prioritize safety by promptly addressing any issues with the power cord.

Managing power usage within your RV is crucial for a hassle-free and safe camping experience. Here are some tips for effective power management:

- **Know your limits:** Understand the power limits of your RV and the campground's electrical supply. Different appliances and systems have varying power requirements. Avoid simultaneously operating high-power appliances that could overload the electrical system.

- **Prioritize essentials:** Identify essential appliances and systems that need continuous power, such as the refrigerator, lighting, and heating or cooling systems. Use these strategically while minimizing the use of non-essential devices.

- **Use energy-efficient appliances:** Consider using energy-efficient appliances and LED lighting to reduce overall power consumption.

- **Unplug when not in use:** Unplug devices or appliances when they're not in use to prevent any standby power drain.

- **Spread out usage:** If possible, stagger the use of high-power devices. For example, avoid using the microwave while the air conditioner is running.

- **Consider alternate power sources:** Utilize propane for heating or cooking, which reduces reliance on electrical systems.

- **Educate everyone:** Ensure everyone staying in the RV understands the importance of power management to prevent accidental overloads.

Balancing the use of appliances and systems ensures that you don't exceed the RV's electrical capacity, preventing potential electrical issues or disruptions during your camping trip. Prioritizing power consumption and being mindful of usage contribute to a smoother and safer camping experience.

Tip: Using extension cords in your RV setup can be necessary at times, but it's essential to do so safely. Use heavy-duty extension cords that are specifically designed for outdoor use and are properly rated for the intended amperage. This ensures they can handle the electrical load without overheating or causing hazards.

While extension cords can be useful, try to limit their use whenever possible. Relying too heavily on extension cords can increase the risk of tripping or damage to the cords, posing potential safety risks. Inspect extension cords before each use for any signs of wear, damage, or fraying. Replace damaged cords immediately to prevent safety hazards.

Use the shortest length of cord necessary to reach the power source. Longer cords can lead to voltage drops, affecting the efficiency of electrical devices. Unplug extension cords when the connected devices are not in use to prevent any potential hazards or accidental trips. Store extension cords properly when not in use to prevent damage or tangling, ensuring they remain in good condition for future use.

Remember, while extension cords can provide temporary solutions, they should not be a permanent fix for electrical connections. Whenever possible, prioritize direct connections and use extension cords as a temporary measure. Understanding your RV's power needs, using adapters when required, and following safe connection practices contribute to a reliable and secure electrical setup during your camping adventures.

Water Connections

When it comes to the RV's water system, there are two types: pressurized and non-pressurized systems. Pressurized systems involve connecting a hose directly to a water source at the campground, providing a constant water supply to the RV's plumbing system.

Non-pressurized systems involve filling the RV's fresh water tank manually and using an onboard water pump for distribution.

Pressurized Water Systems

Setting up your RV's water system is a key factor in ensuring a seamless camping experience. Let's break it down for you so you can confidently navigate the ins and outs of connecting to water sources at campgrounds.

First off, grab yourself a potable water hose to link your RV's water inlet to the campground's water source. Make sure it's not just any hose but one marked safe for drinking water, and secure that connection tight to avoid any unwanted leaks.

Your RV comes equipped with a water inlet, usually hanging out on the exterior. That's where you'll be plugging in the water hose from the campground. Keep an eye out for valves or levers on the inlet; they'll be your go-to for controlling the flow of water into your RV's plumbing system.

Quick tip for your RVing journey: Go for a 100-foot freshwater hose labeled specifically for "freshwater." It might cost a bit more than the 50-foot option, but trust me, you'll thank yourself later. Opt for the collapsible kind to save some storage space. And don't forget to snag a filter and maybe a water regulator. Campgrounds love their high water pressure, which is great, but not all RVs can handle it. I once had a leaky water connection that I couldn't fix despite adding plumber's tape. It was all due to the water pressure in that specific campground before I got my hands on a water pressure regulator.

Speaking of the water pressure regulator, insert that baby between your water source and the RV to keep the water pressure in check.

It's like a shield, protecting your RV's plumbing from potential damage caused by too much pressure at the campground.

Consider throwing in some inline filters into the water hose; they work wonders by clearing out impurities like sediment and contaminants, ensuring your water is top-notch.

Once everything's hooked up, your pressurized water system is good to go, supplying water to all the nooks and crannies inside your RV. It might even include an onboard water pump to help the water flow smoothly to your faucets, sinks, showers, and toilets scattered throughout your RV. Now you're armed with the know-how to make your water connection hassle-free, guaranteeing a comfy and worry-free stay at the campground.

Non-Pressurized Systems

Getting your RV ready for a self-contained adventure without a pressurized water hookup involves several essential steps for a seamless water management experience. Start by filling your RV's fresh water tank, ensuring a self-contained water supply when a pressurized hookup isn't available. Once filled, activate the RV's water pump to pressurize the system, allowing water to be drawn from the freshwater tank and distributed to faucets and appliances within the RV.

To extend your fresh water supply throughout your stay, practice water conservation measures. Regularly inspect water connections for any signs of leaks or damage, addressing issues promptly to prevent unnecessary water waste. Periodically sanitize the fresh water tank to maintain water quality and ensure it remains safe for use.

When it comes to wastewater disposal, handle gray water—waste from sinks and showers—through designated campground facilities or suitable disposal areas. For blackwater from the toilet, connect the sewer hose to the RV's black water tank outlet and link it to the campground's sewage system or dump station for proper disposal.

It's crucial to use a drinking-water-safe hose for freshwater connections to guarantee the quality of the water entering your RV. In colder climates, take precautions to prevent hoses and tanks from freezing by insulating them or using heated hoses. Keep a close eye on tank levels, especially when boondocking without hookups, and plan your water usage accordingly.

Lastly, follow the manufacturer's guidelines for using and maintaining your RV's water heater to ensure a steady supply of hot water. Properly connecting and managing water in your RV is vital to guaranteeing a reliable supply for your daily needs while camping, enhancing your overall comfort and convenience throughout your outdoor adventures.

Sewage Connections

When it comes to sewage connections during your RV camping adventure, it's crucial to prioritize cleanliness for a comfortable and hygienic experience. Grab a designated sewage hose that securely fits your RV's outlet and the campground's dump station. Make sure that the connection is tight and sealed to avoid any unwanted leaks or spills while you're taking care of your business. Always stick to campground rules, and use the designated dump station, wearing gloves and keeping things clean to minimize any risk of contamination.

Start by connecting one end of a specialized sewer hose to your RV's sewage outlet, making sure it's securely attached to prevent any leaks. Place the other end into the campground's dump station or designated sewage receptacle. Remember to empty the black water tank first, followed by the gray water tank, to flush out any lingering gray water and keep your hose clean.

Let me share a little personal wisdom here—RV problems are inevitable. Take a deep breath, be patient, and consider the story of when my RV's black water release valve got stuck open. Instead of panicking, a temporary fix was found with a gate valve pipe extender kit. This is why it's smart to invest in a gate valve before you find yourself in a similar situation. They're not something you can easily replace in the middle of nowhere.

Now, when you're dealing with sewage connections, don't cut corners. Use a dedicated, top-quality sewer hose made specifically for RVs to prevent leaks and accidents. Consider throwing on some disposable gloves for handling the hose and connections, and be sure to sanitize your hands afterward. To keep things smelling fresh, use specialized tank treatments or deodorizers that break down waste inside the tanks.

Make a habit of regularly cleaning and sanitizing your sewer hose and storage compartment to prevent any unpleasant odors. Keep an eye on tank levels, especially during longer stays or when you're off-grid without hookups. And be a good camper—know the specific rules at your campground and any local regulations regarding sewage disposal.

Always double-check that the connection between your RV and the dump station is tight and secure to avoid leaks. Take it easy and follow the proper procedures to prevent spills or leaks. Managing sewage connections in your RV isn't the most glamorous part of the adventure, but it ensures a clean and comfortable environment for you and your fellow campers throughout your trip, all while staying in line with campground rules.

Managing Power and Water Resources

Efficiently managing power and water resources is paramount for a seamless and enjoyable RV camping adventure. Opt for LED lights, unplug idle appliances, and make the most of natural light to cut down on power consumption. Consider investing in energy-efficient appliances and electronics to keep power usage to a minimum.

When it comes to generators, use them judiciously, keeping in mind quiet hours and campground regulations. Only use generators when necessary to recharge batteries or power essential appliances. Enhance water conservation by installing low-flow faucets and showerheads. This not only reduces water usage, but ensures comfort is not compromised.

Mindful water usage extends to activities like dishwashing and showering. Embrace navy showers—wet, turn off, soap up, and rinse—to conserve water. Additionally, repurpose gray water from sinks and showers for tasks like flushing the toilet or watering plants, adhering to regulations. Regularly monitor water and power levels through tank monitoring systems or manual checks to prevent unexpected shortages.

Encourage everyone in the RV to adopt resource-conserving habits to extend available supplies. Always carry extra water and fuel for generators in case of unforeseen shortages or emergencies. Plan for self-sufficiency in remote areas with limited amenities by ensuring extra water and sufficient power reserves.

Calculating power needs and water usage for the entire trip is essential to avoid running out of vital resources. Conservation not only minimizes environmental impact but also helps preserve the natural beauty and ecosystems of camping locations. Efficient resource management ensures a more comfortable camping experience, avoiding discomfort due to shortages.

By incorporating these strategies and staying vigilant about resource levels, campers can maintain a comfortable and eco-friendly camping lifestyle, even in remote or extended camping scenarios.

TROUBLESHOOTING COMMON UTILITY ISSUES

Embarking on RV adventures can sometimes mean facing unexpected challenges with power, water, or sewage systems. In this section, we'll tackle the common hurdles faced by RVers: power outages that dim your experience, pesky water leaks, and the hassle of blocked sewage lines. We're here to guide you through step-by-step solutions for diagnosing and resolving these issues, ensuring your camping journey remains smooth. Additionally, we'll equip you with a checklist of essential tools and supplies—a trusty arsenal to conquer any unexpected bumps on the road. Let's dive in and prepare you to handle these utility hiccups like a pro!

Power Outages

Step 1: Check the electrical pedestal:

1. Safety First: Ensure the RV is disconnected from the power source.
2. Locate the campground's electrical pedestal.
3. Inspect for any breakers that might be in the "off" position or any visible blown fuses.

Step 2: RV's main breaker panel:

1. Go inside the RV to access the main breaker panel.
2. Scan the panel for any tripped breakers—look for switches, not in the "on" position.
3. If a breaker is tripped, firmly switch it off and then back on.

Step 3: Power cord connections:

1. Carefully examine the power cord.
2. Inspect the connections for any loose or damaged plugs.
3. Ensure there are no exposed wires or fraying on the cord.

Step 4: Resetting breakers and fuses:

1. If breakers are found tripped at the electrical pedestal, reset them by switching to the "on" position.
2. If fuses are blown, replace them with new ones of the correct rating.

Step 5: RV's main breaker reset:

1. For any tripped breakers in the RV's main panel, switch them off and back on.
2. Confirm that all switches are securely in the "on" position.

Step 6: Power cord reconnection:

1. If loose or damaged plugs were identified, resecure or replace the power cord as necessary.
2. Ensure all connections are firmly attached and free of damage.

Note: If troubleshooting these steps doesn't restore power or if there are visible signs of damage to the power cord, it may require professional inspection or replacement.

Essential tools:

- Flashlight
- Electrical gloves (optional but recommended for safety)
- Spare fuses (matching the amp rating of the original ones)
- Electrical tape

Always prioritize safety when dealing with electrical systems. If you're unsure or uncomfortable with electrical work, it's advisable to seek assistance from a qualified professional.

Water Leaks

Step 1: Locate the leak source:

1. Visual inspection: Look for signs of water accumulation or dripping.
2. Focus on plumbing fixtures, connections, and areas with water access (sinks, faucets, water heaters, and toilets).

Step 2: Check fittings and connections:

1. Examine all visible pipes, hoses, and fittings for any signs of moisture or pooling water.
2. Look for loose connections, damaged pipes, or worn-out seals.

Step 3: Tightening fittings and connections:

1. If a leak is traced to a loose connection, gently tighten it using the appropriate tools.
2. Avoid overtightening, as it might cause damage or worsen the issue.

Step 4: Replacing damaged parts:

1. Identify any damaged or worn-out components contributing to the leak.
2. Replace these parts with new ones that match the specifications of the original components.

Step 5: Temporary sealant application:

1. If immediate replacement or repair isn't feasible, use waterproof sealant or tape as a temporary fix.
2. Apply the sealant or tape over the leak source, ensuring a tight and secure seal.

Note: While temporary fixes may alleviate the immediate issue, permanent repairs or replacements should be made as soon as possible to prevent further leaks.

Essential tools:

- Adjustable wrench or appropriate tools for tightening connections
- Pipe tape or sealant (for temporary fixes)
- Replacement parts (e.g., fittings, seals) if needed

Be cautious when dealing with water sources and plumbing. If the leak persists after attempting these steps or if it involves complex internal plumbing, seeking professional assistance is recommended to avoid exacerbating the problem.

Blocked Sewage Lines

Step 1: Identifying signs of blockage:

1. Observation: Look for backups in sinks, showers, or toilets—slow-draining or standing water.
2. Listen for unusual gurgling sounds when using sinks or showers, indicating air bubbles trapped in the blockage.

Step 2: Flushing the sewer hose:

1. Use a sewer hose flushing attachment designed to dislodge minor blockages.
2. Attach the flushing tool to the sewer hose and apply water pressure to push debris or clogs through the line.

Step 3: Utilizing sewer line cleaners:

1. Choose an appropriate sewer line cleaner or enzyme-based cleaner from a camping supply store.
2. Follow the product instructions to pour the recommended amount into the sewage system.
3. These cleaners break down obstructions, aiding in the clearance of blockages over time.

Step 4: Using a plumber's snake:

1. For persistent or stubborn clogs, use a plumber's snake (auger).
2. Carefully insert the snake into the drain or cleanout port and rotate it to dislodge and remove blockages.

Note: Always follow safety guidelines and instructions when using plumbing tools or chemicals.

Essential tools and supplies:

- Sewer hose flushing attachment
- Sewer line cleaner or enzyme-based cleaner
- Plumber's snake (auger)
- Protective gloves and eyewear

For extensive or persistent blockages that cannot be resolved using these methods, seeking professional assistance from a plumber or RV service provider is advisable to prevent further complications or damage to the RV's sewage system.

Once you are well-versed in hookups and utilities, the next thrilling phase is journey planning. The upcoming chapter,

"Navigation and Travel Planning," illustrates the importance of meticulous planning for a smooth and delightful RV adventure. Efficient planning paves the way for unforgettable journeys filled with exploration and wonder.

CHAPTER 6

NAVIGATING AND TRAVEL PLANNING

Navigating an RV demands more than a map; it's about transforming a journey into a full-fledged adventure through smart decisions and informed choices. This chapter is your compass, your guide to mastering the art of navigation and travel planning in RV exploration. Get ready to uncover essential tools and gain insightful tips for orchestrating successful and memorable RV adventures.

PLANNING YOUR ROUTE: TOOLS AND TIPS

Planning your RV route involves several essential steps to ensure a smooth and enjoyable journey. Considerations like road size, height restrictions, and scenic value play a crucial role in crafting your travel itinerary.

Assessing Road Conditions: Roadwear Fashion Check

Opt for roads that fit your RV like a glove, avoiding narrow or winding routes that could turn your drive into a headache. The goal is to find roads that comfortably accommodate your RV's size and weight, creating a smoother and more enjoyable journey. By assessing road conditions, you pave the way for a stress-free adventure.

Height and Clearance: Dodge the Duck and Cover Moments

Ever had a "duck and cover" moment in your RV? Avoid surprises by being vigilant about bridges, tunnels, and areas with potential height restrictions. Safeguard your RV's rooftop from unexpected rearrangements by double-checking that your rig glides through these spaces without any unwelcome modifications. Height and clearance awareness ensure a smooth and incident-free journey.

Scenic Routes: Transform Your Drive Into a Moving Postcard

Why settle for a mundane journey when you can turn it into a moving postcard? Opt for scenic byways and routes that offer breathtaking views, transforming your drive into a visual feast. These scenic routes not only add aesthetic pleasure to your journey but also create memorable moments that linger long after the adventure concludes. Elevate your RV experience with routes that delight the eyes and soothe the soul.

Thinking about these planning steps as your roadmap sets the stage for a smoother and more enjoyable adventure. It's akin to choosing the best path to ensure your RV journey is not only picturesque but also stress-free. By carefully considering road conditions, height and clearance factors, and incorporating scenic routes, you're laying the foundation for an RV adventure filled with scenic wonders and delightful discoveries.

When it comes to route planning for your RV adventure, having the right resources can make a world of difference. Here's a closer look at some essential tools to ensure a smooth and enjoyable journey.

Digital Apps: Roadtrippers and RV Trip Wizard

When it comes to planning your RV journey, Roadtrippers and RV Trip Wizard stand out as indispensable digital travel companions. Let's delve into the details of these dynamic apps:

Roadtrippers is not your run-of-the-mill navigation app—it's your passport to a personalized and enriching travel experience. Beyond the basic function of getting you from point A to point B, Roadtrippers adds a layer of excitement to your journey. Think of it as having a savvy local guide who knows all the hidden gems and scenic spots along the way. This app tailors routes to your preferences, ensuring that every stretch of road is an opportunity for discovery. Whether you're into quirky roadside attractions, picturesque viewpoints, or charming towns, Roadtrippers guides you to the extraordinary, making your RV adventure a truly unique and memorable experience.

RV Trip Wizard takes route planning to a whole new level, specially designed for the RV enthusiast. This app considers the intricacies of your RV, such as size and safety requirements, and provides routes specifically crafted for larger vehicles. Imagine having a virtual co-pilot that not only guides you through RV-friendly routes but also alerts you about potential challenges like low-clearance areas. RV Trip Wizard ensures a stress-free and enjoyable journey, helping you navigate with confidence. Additionally, it assists in locating suitable campgrounds or rest stops along the way, ensuring that your route aligns perfectly with your RVing needs.

Google Maps remains a classic choice for good reason. This familiar interface offers detailed navigation and real-time traffic updates, ensuring that your RV journey is not only convenient but also free from unnecessary hassles. While it might lack some RV-specific features, its user-friendly design and comprehensive mapping capabilities make it a reliable companion for a hassle-free trip.

Roadtrippers and RV Trip Wizard go beyond being mere navigation tools—they are your virtual travel guides, enhancing your journey with tailored routes, hidden gems, and unique stops. Meanwhile, Google Maps, a timeless choice, ensures seamless navigation with its familiar interface. Together, these apps form a trio of essential tools, ensuring that your RV adventure is not just a trip but a curated experience filled with exploration and delight.

Maps: The Classic and the Digital

In planning for your RV adventure, maps play a pivotal role, and whether you prefer the classic charm of paper or the modern convenience of digital, each brings its own unique touch to the journey.

There's a certain magic in unfolding a paper map, tracing your finger along the routes, and feeling the tangible connection to your journey. Classic paper maps evoke a sense of nostalgia, reminiscent of a time when unfolding a map was an integral part of the adventure. The tactile appeal of a paper map adds an extra layer of engagement to your route planning, making it a hands-on and immersive experience. It's like holding a piece of history in your hands as you navigate the roads.

In the age of technology, digital maps bring a level of convenience that's hard to ignore. With just a few taps, you can zoom in for a closer look at specific routes, points of interest, and potential stops along the way. The real-time updates offered by digital maps ensure that you're equipped with the latest information, making your journey not just planned but adaptable to changing conditions. The ease of carrying an entire map database in your pocket is a game-changer, especially when navigating through complex road networks or exploring unfamiliar territories.

Whether you opt for the classic appeal of paper maps or the digital prowess of modern counterparts, maps serve as your guiding companions on the road. They provide a bird's-eye view of your route, allowing you to spot potential detours and discover scenic byways. The choice between classic and digital is a matter of personal preference, with each offering its own unique charm and functionality.

In essence, maps are more than just navigational tools; they're gateways to exploration and discovery. So, whether you're unfolding a paper map with a sense of nostalgia or swiping across a digital screen for real-time insights, embrace the journey and let the maps lead you to the next exciting chapter of your RV adventure.

RV-Specific GPS Systems: Your Virtual Co-Pilot

When it comes to navigating the open road with your RV, having a virtual co-pilot who understands the unique needs of your rig can make all the difference. Enter RV-specific GPS systems, tailor-made to elevate your route planning and ensure a stress-free and enjoyable journey.

These dedicated GPS systems go beyond the capabilities of standard navigation tools. They are specifically designed with your RV in mind, considering factors such as size, weight, and safety requirements. This means that the routes they suggest are curated to accommodate the dimensions of larger vehicles, ensuring a smooth and safe journey.

One standout feature of RV-specific GPS systems is their ability to keep you informed about potential challenges along your route. Imagine approaching a low-clearance area, and your virtual co-pilot alerts you well in advance. It's like having a second set of eyes focused on the road, helping you navigate with confidence and avoid unexpected obstacles that could put a damper on your adventure.

These systems don't just guide you from point A to point B. They enrich your travel experience by providing valuable information about suitable campgrounds and rest stops along your route. Need a break or a place to spend the night? Your virtual co-pilot has got you covered, ensuring that your journey is not only safe but also comfortable and convenient.

Think of RV-specific GPS systems as your trusty road trip ally. They contribute to a stress-free navigation experience, allowing you to focus on the scenery and enjoy the ride. With these systems on board, you're not just reaching your destination, you're making the entire journey a delightful and memorable part of your RV adventure.

Whether you're embracing the tech-savvy approach with digital apps or savoring the classic charm of paper maps, adding an RV-specific GPS to your travel toolkit ensures a well-rounded and enhanced road trip. It's the assurance that every turn is RV-friendly, every stop is well-informed, and every mile is part of an unforgettable journey.

Rest Stops: More Than Just a Pause

You're cruising down the open road in your RV, the miles rolling beneath your wheels. During this journey, strategically placed rest stops become more than just a pause; they are essential oases contributing to the rhythm of your adventure. Rest stops aren't just about giving your legs a stretch—although that's a perk too. They are strategically planned interludes designed to unleash a wave of comfort and focus during your journey. These mini-breaks are your secret weapon against the monotony of the road, ensuring that you stay sharp and engaged.

Picture stepping out of your RV into the open air, surrounded by the sights and sounds of nature. It's a moment to refresh your mind and unwind your senses. Take a stroll, breathe in the invigorating fresh air, and let the surroundings work their magic. These brief respites not only reenergize your body but also rejuvenate your spirit for the road ahead. Beyond immediate comfort, incorporating rest stops into your route planning significantly enhances safety and enjoyment. A well-timed break allows you to reset, combat fatigue, and maintain focus. It's a simple yet powerful strategy to ensure that every mile of your journey is not just covered but embraced with enthusiasm.

Rest stops often come with the bonus of stunning scenery. Imagine pulling over to a viewpoint that unveils nature's masterpiece—a panorama of mountains, a lakeside retreat, or a sun-kissed meadow. These visual feasts turn your rest stops into memorable moments, adding layers of beauty to your travel narrative. Rest stops are the threads that weave comfort into the fabric of your journey. They break up the drive into chapters, each marked by a moment of relaxation and appreciation. Embrace them not just as breaks but as essential components of an enjoyable and safe travel experience.

So, as you plan your route, consider the strategic placement of these restful havens. Let each rest stop be more than just a pause— let it be a purposeful punctuation in your road trip story. After all, the joy of the journey lies not just in reaching the destination but in savoring every moment along the way.

Enjoyable Travel: Spice Up Your Adventure

Step off the beaten path and schedule stops at quirky roadside attractions that defy the ordinary. These offbeat gems inject a sense of playfulness into your journey, creating moments that linger in your memory long after the road trip is over. Whether it's the world's largest ball of yarn or a museum dedicated to peculiar artifacts, these stops turn your adventure into a whimsical treasure hunt.

Take your travel experience to new heights—literally! Schedule stops at breathtaking viewpoints along your route. Imagine pulling over to witness a sunrise painting the sky in hues of orange and pink or gazing at a panoramic vista of rolling hills and endless horizons. These scenic interludes transform your road trip into a visual feast, creating snapshots of awe inspiring beauty.

Venture beyond the highway and explore charming towns tucked away along your route. These quaint havens often hold hidden gems—local eateries, artisan shops, or historical landmarks waiting to be discovered. Stroll through cobblestone streets, savor local flavors, and immerse yourself in the unique character of each town. It's a delightful way to break up the drive and connect with the heart of your chosen route.

Leave room for the unexpected. Embrace spontaneity as a guiding principle of your journey. Allow yourself to deviate from the planned route if a roadside sign piques your interest or if a hidden trail beckons. It's in these unplanned moments that the true essence of adventure reveals itself, creating stories that unfold organically and become cherished chapters of your travel narrative.

By incorporating enjoyable detours into your road trip, you're not just covering miles; you're creating lasting memories. These moments of spontaneity become the ultimate souvenirs of your adventure. Whether it's a laughter-filled pit stop at a roadside oddity or a quiet moment of reflection at a scenic overlook, each detour adds depth and vibrancy to your travel experience.

So, as you plan your adventure, let spontaneity be your co-pilot. Schedule stops that promise fun, discovery, and a touch of the unexpected. Turn your road trip into a kaleidoscope of experiences, where every twist and turn brings a new and delightful surprise. After all, the joy of travel lies in the journey itself.

Overnight Campgrounds: Plan and Book Ahead

As you navigate the winding roads of your RV adventure, the prospect of a tranquil overnight stay becomes a crucial part of the journey. Here's why planning and booking your campground ahead of time is the key to unlocking a restful and stress-free night under the stars.

Have a curated list of potential overnight stays tailored to your preferences. By researching campgrounds in advance, you gain insight into the diverse options available along your route. From secluded spots immersed in nature's serenity to well-equipped RV parks offering modern conveniences, this proactive approach empowers you to choose the perfect setting for your night's rest. By booking ahead, you eliminate the uncertainty of searching for available spaces, especially during peak travel times. This assurance not only provides peace of mind but also allows you to relax and unwind, knowing that your overnight sanctuary is secured.

Every traveler has unique preferences when it comes to campground amenities. Some seek the tranquility of a secluded site, while others appreciate the convenience of full hookups and facilities. Planning enables you to handpick campgrounds that align with your specific needs, ensuring a tailored experience that complements your travel style.

Navigating unfamiliar terrain to find a suitable campground can be a stressful end to a day of exploration. When you plan and book in advance, you sidestep the guesswork. Your route is clear, and your chosen campground is a known destination, streamlining the arrival process and allowing you to settle in swiftly for a relaxing evening.

After a day of scenic drives and memorable stops, a serene night under the stars awaits you. By planning and booking ahead, you've not only secured a comfortable resting place but also set the stage for an immersive experience with nature. Whether you choose a site surrounded by towering trees or a location with a panoramic view of the night sky, the tranquility of your chosen campground becomes the ultimate reward for your meticulous planning.

In essence, planning and booking your overnight campgrounds in advance transforms your RV journey into a seamlessly orchestrated adventure. It's a proactive step that ensures optimal comfort, peace of mind, and the opportunity to savor the beauty of each chosen overnight haven. So, as you embark on your road trip, let the anticipation of a well-planned night's stay be a guiding beacon, illuminating the path to a restful and rejuvenating experience.

Strive for the perfect balance between driving and exploring. While reaching your destination is undoubtedly the goal, remember that the journey itself is an adventure. Resist the urge to rush through it; instead, take your time to absorb the beauty and cultural richness of the places you encounter along the way. A well-paced journey not only reduces stress but also allows you to fully appreciate the diverse landscapes and experiences that unfold before you.

Incorporating these tips into your travel strategy ensures that your RV adventure is not just about the destination but also about the joyous moments and discoveries along the way. Whether it's a well-timed rest stop, a spontaneous detour, a pre-booked campground, or a leisurely exploration, each element contributes to a smoother and more delightful journey. Safe travels!

NAVIGATING WITH AN RV OR WHILE TOWING

Navigating with an RV or while towing requires a unique approach due to the size and weight of the vehicle, demanding careful attention to various challenges for a safe and smooth journey.

Turning Radius

Maneuvering a larger vehicle, such as an RV or a trailer, necessitates a grasp of its turning radius due to its size and weight distribution. Unlike smaller vehicles, RVs and trailers have a significantly wider turning radius, requiring more space to negotiate turns effectively.

RVs and trailers have an extended wheelbase, making turns in tight spaces more challenging. This elongated wheelbase means the vehicle's rear wheels take a wider path than those of a standard car when turning. Understanding this crucial aspect will help you anticipate the necessary space required to execute turns safely and avoid potential collisions with curbs, obstacles, or other vehicles.

The best way to enhance your familiarity with the vehicle's turning radius is by practicing wider turns in an open space, such as an empty parking lot or an unoccupied road. This exercise allows you to gauge the vehicle's swing and better comprehend the space needed to navigate turns smoothly without impacting nearby objects.

When approaching a turn, especially in confined spaces, you should initiate the turn earlier than you might with a smaller vehicle. This early initiation allows the vehicle's rear to clear any obstacles or curbs effectively. Additionally, utilizing the entirety of the available road space while making the turn can minimize the risk of the vehicle encroaching onto adjacent lanes or objects.

Maintaining constant awareness of the vehicle's dimensions is essential, particularly when turning. You should be mindful of potential blind spots, using side mirrors and rearview cameras where available, to monitor the vehicle's movement and surrounding obstacles.

Understanding the unique turning capabilities of an RV or trailer and practicing wider turns in safe environments can significantly enhance your ability to navigate the vehicle safely, mitigating the risk of accidents or collisions while maneuvering in tighter spaces.

Clearance Issues

Height and width restrictions are crucial factors to consider, especially with bridges, tunnels, or low-hanging structures along the route. Detailed route planning is essential to avoid areas that may pose clearance issues for the vehicle. Researching and selecting routes that accommodate the size without any height or width restrictions is vital for smooth navigation.

RVs and trailers come in various heights and widths, each having specific clearance requirements. Researching and understanding the vehicle's exact dimensions is important to identify potential clearance hazards along the planned route.

Thorough route planning is essential to circumvent areas with height or width limitations that the vehicle cannot accommodate. Leveraging online resources, specialized RV GPS systems or travel guides can aid in identifying routes that suit the vehicle's dimensions without any clearance restrictions.

Bridges, overpasses, tunnels, and even some gas station canopies may have height limitations. A careful review of these potential obstacles allows for the selection of routes that steer clear of structures too low for the vehicle's height.

Narrow passages, roadways with limited width, or areas where vehicles are required to navigate within confined lanes can pose challenges for wider RVs or trailers. Selecting routes that provide adequate width for the vehicle without encroaching into adjacent lanes or obstacles is essential.

When on the road, vigilance is key. Signage indicating height or width limitations should be diligently observed. Additionally, using RV-specific GPS systems or apps that offer real-time updates on potential clearance issues can be beneficial.

By conducting detailed route planning and research before the journey, you can ensure they select paths free from height or width restrictions that might impede the vehicle's passage. This meticulous planning helps prevent unexpected detours, ensuring a smoother and safer travel experience.

Slow Speeds

With RVs and trailers, you usually have to travel at slower speeds, affecting travel time and overall road dynamics. Driving at a reduced pace necessitates patience and mindfulness of speed limits, ensuring safety on the road. It's essential to maintain a safe distance from other vehicles, especially when slower speeds might affect traffic flow.

Slower speeds demand a shift in driving habits and mindset. Maintaining patience becomes crucial, especially when traveling on highways or through areas with faster-moving traffic. Accepting the slower pace and being prepared for longer travel durations is essential for a stress-free journey.

Maintaining a safe distance from other vehicles is critical when driving at slower speeds. This practice ensures sufficient reaction time and minimizes the risk of rear-end collisions, particularly on highways or busy roads where traffic flow might be faster.

Respecting posted speed limits is imperative for road safety, regardless of the vehicle's speed capacity. Being mindful of and adhering to speed regulations not only ensures compliance with the law but also contributes to safer travel conditions for all road users.

Slower speeds can impact the overall traffic flow. To mitigate disruptions, particularly on highways or multi-lane roads, it's advisable to maintain awareness of surrounding traffic and move into slower traffic lanes whenever feasible to allow faster-moving vehicles to pass safely.

While slower speeds may extend travel time, they can also contribute to a more comfortable and relaxed journey. It allows for better control of the vehicle, reduces fuel consumption, and offers a chance to appreciate the scenic beauty along the way.

Embracing a patient and attentive approach to driving is key. Being alert, focused, and patient while navigating at reduced speeds ensures a safer and more enjoyable travel experience for both the driver and fellow road users.

By acknowledging and adapting to the implications of slower speeds, RV and trailer drivers can navigate roads safely, effectively manage travel time, and contribute to a more harmonious flow of traffic while enjoying their journey.

BEST PRACTICES FOR SAFE AND ENJOYABLE TRAVEL

Navigating with an RV or while towing necessitates a distinct approach due to the size, weight, and handling characteristics of these vehicles. To ensure a safe and smooth journey, it's essential to adopt specific strategies.

Constant vigilance is vital for safe navigation. Utilize side mirrors effectively to monitor surrounding traffic and maintain awareness of adjacent lanes. Staying attentive to the road ahead helps anticipate potential hazards, abrupt turns, or lane changes by other vehicles.

Accept and adapt to the slower pace required when driving larger vehicles, especially in congested urban areas or unfamiliar terrain. Hastily maneuvering a sizeable RV or towing a trailer through such conditions increases the risk of accidents. Embrace a patient approach to maneuvering and navigating, allowing ample time for turns, lane changes, or merging onto highways.

Conducting thorough pre-trip inspections is paramount. Ensure critical components like brakes, lights, tires, and towing equipment are in optimal condition. This proactive approach minimizes the likelihood of unexpected breakdowns or system failures during the journey, enhancing overall safety and reliability.

Anticipate and address the challenges posed by larger vehicles. Familiarize yourself with the turning radius and handling characteristics of the RV or trailer. Practice wider turns in open spaces to gain confidence and prevent collisions with curbs or obstacles.

Maintain a heightened level of awareness while driving. Larger vehicles have blind spots, so constantly scanning and being mindful of blind spots can prevent accidents caused by unseen vehicles or obstacles.

Equip yourself with the knowledge and skills to handle unexpected situations. Learn how to respond to system failures, tire blowouts, or emergency stops, ensuring you're ready to manage potential crises effectively.

When it comes to safe and enjoyable travel in an RV or while towing, a few key practices can make a world of difference:

1. Weather forecasts

Checking weather conditions before hitting the road is crucial. Stay updated on forecasts along your route to anticipate any potential challenges. Be prepared for rain, snow, or adverse weather that might affect driving conditions. Adjust your itinerary if necessary to avoid weather-related risks and ensure a safer journey.

2. Understanding weight distribution

Proper weight distribution in your RV or trailer is like maintaining balance in a tightrope walk. Ensure heavier items are evenly distributed and properly secured. Balanced weight helps maintain stability, preventing issues like swaying or loss of control while driving. Regularly check and adjust the weight distribution to ensure optimal handling.

3. Enhancing the travel experience

Beyond simply getting from point A to point B, embrace the journey itself. Choose scenic routes to immerse yourself in natural beauty. Consider detours to visit local landmarks, explore hidden gems, or take short hikes to break the monotony of the drive. These stops not only add joy to your journey but also create lasting memories.

4. Sustainable and respectful travel

Being a responsible traveler is essential. Leave no trace at your campsites—pack out what you pack in and dispose of waste properly. Adhere to campground regulations, respect wildlife, and honor local customs and cultures. By practicing sustainable travel, you help preserve the environment and contribute positively to the communities you visit.

Incorporating these practices isn't just about personal comfort and safety; it's about being a conscientious traveler. Prioritizing safety, enjoyment, and sustainability not only enriches your travel experience but also contributes to the preservation of the natural and cultural richness of the places you explore.

While successful navigation and travel planning are pivotal, they're mere parts of the RVing experience. The upcoming chapter, "Maintenance, Storage, and Security," underscores the significance of maintaining and securing the RV—ensuring that all the meticulous planning culminates in a rewarding and stress-free adventure.

CHAPTER 7

MAINTENANCE, STORAGE, AND SECURITY

Keeping your RV in top-notch condition and ensuring its security are paramount for a smooth and enjoyable journey. A well-maintained RV can endure for decades, becoming your faithful travel companion. Yet, neglecting regular maintenance can turn into a costly affair, shortening its lifespan significantly. Regular care not only saves money but also ensures safety and reliability on the road.

In this chapter, you'll discover a treasure trove of tips and strategies dedicated to the care, storage, and security of your RV. Whether you're a seasoned traveler or just starting your RV adventures, these insights will prove invaluable. Learn the ropes of regular maintenance, from checking tires and brakes to inspecting electrical systems. Discover how routine checks and proactive care can prevent unexpected breakdowns, ensuring your RV remains road-ready.

Uncover the secrets to proper RV storage—whether it's for the winter months or during off-seasons. Protect your investment by learning how to safeguard it from the elements, pests, and potential damage while not in use. Dive into foolproof methods to secure your RV against theft or unauthorized access. Explore techniques to safeguard both the vehicle and its contents, ensuring peace of mind while you're exploring the great outdoors or taking a well-deserved break.

By mastering these maintenance, storage, and security strategies, you're not just prolonging your RV's life and reliability; you're investing in worry-free adventures, allowing you to focus on making lasting memories on the open road.

REGULAR RV MAINTENANCE TIPS

The best way to maintain your RV is with a routine schedule that ensures it's always ready for your adventures and won't leave you stranded next to the road. Create a checklist for yourself, making sure to include three essential main checks:

- engine
- tires
- system flush

Let's take a closer look at what you need to do and look out for.

Taking good care of your RV is like giving it a spa day—it keeps everything running smoothly and extends its road-tripping lifespan. Here's a down-to-earth guide to keeping your RV in tip-top shape:

Engine Checks

Taking care of your RV's engine is like tending to its heart. It involves a careful examination of belts, hoses, and fluid levels.

The timing belt, responsible for synchronizing engine components, should be scrutinized for cracks or fraying. Similarly, the serpentine belt, which is crucial for various engine functions, must be checked for proper tension and any signs of damage.

Hoses, vital for coolant circulation, need regular inspection for bulges, cracks, or leaks. Timely replacement of worn hoses is paramount to preventing issues down the road.

Maintaining appropriate fluid levels is equally crucial for a healthy engine. Regularly check the engine oil using the dipstick, adhering to the manufacturer's recommended oil type and change intervals.

Keep an eye on the coolant level to ensure it falls within the specified range, and top up with the recommended coolant if necessary. Checking transmission and brake fluid levels is also essential, as low levels can compromise the performance of these critical systems.

When it comes to changing oil and replacing the oil filter, it's a chore that shouldn't be neglected. The frequency of oil changes depends on your RV's mileage, typically ranging between 3,000 and 5,000 miles. Always refer to your rig's manual for precise recommendations. Use the recommended oil grade for your engine type, and consider the special oil requirements that some RVs, particularly those with diesel engines, may have. Remember, changing the oil filter is just as important and should be done concurrently with each oil change. Opt for a quality oil filter to ensure the longevity of your engine.

Air filter maintenance is another key aspect of engine care. Regularly inspect the air filter, especially if traversing dusty terrain, as a clogged filter can hinder engine performance. Replacement schedules vary, but a general guideline is to change the air filter every 12,000 to 15,000 miles. Fortunately, replacing an air filter is often a straightforward DIY task, with specific instructions available in your RV's manual.

By paying attention to these engine maintenance tasks, you're not just ensuring a smooth ride but also extending the life of your RV's engine. So, pop the hood, show that engine some love, and keep the adventures rolling!

Tire Inspections

Before embarking on any adventure, it's crucial to check the tire pressure, including the spare tire. Utilize a reliable pressure gauge and ensure the tires are inflated to the recommended PSI (pounds per square inch) specified in your RV manual. Maintaining the correct pressure is vital for even tire wear and optimal on-road performance. Underinflated tires can lead to increased rolling resistance, affecting fuel efficiency and potentially causing over-heating.

Regularly measuring tire tread depth is essential for assessing tire wear and ensuring safety on the road. Use a tread depth gauge to measure the depth of the tire grooves. Insufficient tread depth compromises traction, particularly in wet or slippery conditions. Consider replacing tires that fall below the recommended tread depth to maintain adequate road grip and prevent hydroplaning. Tires with inadequate tread may also have diminished braking performance.

A comprehensive inspection of your tires goes beyond pressure and tread depth. Examine each tire for signs of damage, bulges, or cracks. Address any visible issues promptly, as these can lead to tire failure and potentially hazardous situations on the road. If you notice irregular wear patterns, it may indicate misalignment or other mechanical issues that warrant professional attention.

If you spot any abnormalities during your visual inspection, consider seeking a professional evaluation. Tire issues can sometimes be indicative of broader problems with your RV's suspension or alignment. Investing time in thorough tire examinations contributes not only to your safety but also to the longevity of your tires, potentially saving you from unexpected roadside setbacks.

Remember, your tires are the literal foundation of your RV's journey. Regular and meticulous inspections ensure they are up to the task, providing you with a reliable and secure ride for all your adventures.

System Flushes

Water System

Maintaining your RV's water system is crucial for both water quality and preventing bacterial growth. Over time, sediments can accumulate, affecting the taste and safety of the water you use. Stagnant water in your RV can also become a breeding ground for bacteria.

To begin the maintenance process, start by draining the fresh water tank completely. Depending on your RV's setup, you can use the built-in drainage system or an external hose. Once drained, it's time to prepare a cleaning solution. You can choose between an

RV-safe cleaning product or a vinegar-based solution. Vinegar is a natural and cost-effective option for breaking down deposits.

Refill the fresh water tank with the chosen cleaning solution. Ensure that the solution runs through all faucets, both hot and cold, reaching every part of the water system. Don't forget about outlets such as the shower, toilet, and any other water sources in your RV.

After completing the flushing process with the cleaning solution, it's time to sanitize the water system. Refer to your RV manual for specific guidelines on preparing a chlorine solution. Typically, this involves mixing a specified amount of household bleach with water. Introduce the chlorine solution into the fresh water tank and allow it to sit for the duration recommended in your RV manual. This gives the chlorine time to disinfect the entire water system.

Once the sitting period is complete, flush the entire system again. Run water through all faucets until you no longer detect the smell of chlorine, ensuring that all residual sanitizing agents are removed.

Establishing a regular maintenance schedule is crucial. Aim to perform this flushing and sanitizing process at least once a season, or more frequently if your RV sees heavy use. Additionally, if your RV is equipped with a water filter, consider replacing it during this maintenance routine to enhance water quality.

Propane System

The propane system in your RV is a vital component, facilitating various functions like cooking and heating. Ensuring its proper functioning is crucial for both convenience and safety, making regular inspections and leak tests essential.

Commence your inspection by thoroughly examining the propane tanks, lines, and connections. Look out for any indications of damage or wear that might compromise the system's integrity. Pay special attention to areas susceptible to rust, dents, or other visible irregularities.

Performing leak tests is a critical aspect of propane system maintenance. To conduct a comprehensive test, prepare a soapy water solution or use a specialized leak detection fluid. Apply the solution to all connections, joints, and areas prone to potential leaks, ensuring complete coverage. Observing the applied areas closely, check for the formation of bubbles, as this indicates a potential leak. The soapy solution reacts with the escaping propane, making bubbles visible.

Should any leaks be identified during your inspection or testing, it is imperative to address them immediately. Ignoring propane leaks can pose serious safety risks, considering propane's highly flammable nature. Promptly tighten loose connections or replace damaged components to mitigate potential hazards.

If you find yourself uncertain or uncomfortable handling propane system issues, it is advisable to seek professional servicing. Certified technicians possess the expertise to conduct comprehensive inspections, identify hidden issues, and perform necessary repairs or replacements. Opting for professional servicing ensures the system's integrity and compliance with safety standards.

Maintaining a proactive approach to your RV's propane system is not just about convenience but, more importantly, about safety. By incorporating regular inspections and leak tests and addressing identified issues promptly, you contribute to a safer and more enjoyable RV experience. Remember, when in doubt, seeking professional assistance is always a prudent choice to guarantee the proper functioning of your propane system.

Sewage System

Maintaining your RV's sewage system is not only crucial for your convenience but also plays a vital role in preventing blockages, unpleasant odors, and potential health hazards. To keep your sewage system in optimal condition, it's essential to follow a few key maintenance practices.

Periodically flushing and maintaining the sewage system are primary tasks in ensuring its proper function. Utilize RV-friendly products specifically designed to break down waste and keep the system clean. These products assist in preventing the buildup of solids and maintaining the overall health of the system.

In addition to using sewage system-friendly products, it's important to conduct regular checks on valves and connections. Look for any signs of leaks or obstructions in the system. This proactive approach allows you to identify and address potential issues before they escalate into messy or inconvenient situations.

A notable feature of numerous high-end RVs is the inclusion of flush systems designed to simplify the cleaning process. With this setup, connecting a hose for a mere 15 minutes can effectively flush out the sewage system. This not only removes waste but also helps prevent the buildup of residue that could lead to unpleasant odors. The convenience of this system makes it a valuable tool for RV owners, streamlining the maintenance routine.

For those without built-in flush systems, there's still a solution to ensure thorough cleaning. Innovative gadgets are available that can be placed directly in the toilet. By connecting these gadgets to a hose, users can achieve a comprehensive cleaning of the sewage system. This alternative method is efficient and offers an additional layer of flexibility for RV owners who may not have access to a built-in flush system.

While maintaining a clean sewage system is important throughout the year, it becomes especially crucial during the summer months. Warmer temperatures can exacerbate any lingering odors, making it imperative to keep the system as clean as possible. The combination of heat and confined spaces in an RV can magnify any unpleasant smells, making regular and thorough cleaning a top priority for a comfortable and enjoyable travel experience.

By adhering to these sewage system maintenance routines, you not only contribute to the longevity of your RV but also enhance your overall travel experience. Regular checks and proactive measures ensure a safer and smoother journey, allowing you to focus on the joy of your adventures without the stress of unexpected breakdowns.

Remember, a well-maintained sewage system is not just about functionality—it's about ensuring a comfortable and hassle-free experience during your travels. So, make these routine checks a part of your RV maintenance schedule and enjoy your adventures with peace of mind.

Importance of Cleaning

Maintaining a clean interior within your RV involves a series of practices geared toward preventing wear and tear and ensuring a comfortable living space. Regular dusting and vacuuming are essential to combat dust buildup on various surfaces, including upholstery and carpets. Utilizing microfiber cloths or appropriate vacuum attachments helps in achieving thorough cleanliness, contributing to a more pleasant interior environment.

Upholstery care is a critical aspect of interior maintenance. Quickly addressing spills and stains is key to preventing long-term damage. Employ suitable cleaners based on the material of your upholstery—be it fabric, leather, or vinyl. Additionally, considering the use of fabric protectors adds an extra layer of defense against stains, ultimately extending the life of your RV's upholstery.

In terms of surface maintenance, wiping down surfaces, countertops, and cabinets with RV-safe cleaning solutions is crucial for a hygienic interior. It's advisable to steer clear of abrasive cleaners that could potentially harm finishes. Paying particular attention to areas prone to moisture or spills, like the kitchen and bathroom, helps prevent the growth of mold or mildew.

Shifting our focus to the exterior, regular washing is a fundamental practice to keep your RV looking fresh and well-maintained. Removing road grime, bugs, and debris accumulated during travel is essential. Opt for mild soap or dedicated RV wash products, employing a soft-bristle brush or sponge. Thoroughly rinsing and drying with a microfiber cloth ensures a spotless exterior and prevents water spots.

Applying protective measures to the exterior, such as wax or sealant, serves more than just aesthetic purposes. This protective layer shields the paint from UV rays and environmental elements, playing a crucial role in preventing oxidation and fading. It is a proactive step in maintaining the overall integrity and appearance of your RV.

Don't overlook the importance of cleaning the roof and awnings. Regular cleaning with specialized products designed for RV roofs and awnings removes dirt, mold, or mildew. This diligent maintenance contributes significantly to the longevity of these components.

Regular cleaning and maintenance are not just about aesthetics— they are essential practices for preserving your RV investment, ensuring a comfortable interior, and guaranteeing an enjoyable travel experience. Whether inside or outside, a clean RV is a happy RV.

SEASONAL MAINTENANCE: PRE-SEASON AND OFF-SEASON CHECKS

Seasonal maintenance is a vital aspect of keeping your RV in peak condition year-round. It involves a comprehensive approach to ensure that all systems are functioning correctly and that your RV is ready for the challenges each season brings.

Pre-Season Checks

Before embarking on your RV adventures during the peak travel season, it's crucial to conduct thorough checks on the HVAC, electrical, and plumbing systems to ensure a trouble-free journey.

HVAC Systems

Inspect and test the heating, ventilation, and air conditioning (HVAC) systems. This includes checking the functionality of both the heating and cooling components. Verify that your RV's interior climate control systems are operating efficiently, providing comfort throughout your travels.

Electrical Components

Examine all electrical components within your RV. This encompasses lights, outlets, and appliances. Ensure that each element is in proper working order to guarantee a well-lit and fully functional living space. A comprehensive electrical check minimizes the risk of unexpected disruptions during your trips.

Plumbing System

Take the time to inspect the plumbing system for any potential issues. Look for leaks or damaged pipes that could lead to problems during your travels. A meticulous examination of the plumbing ensures that your water supply remains intact, preventing inconvenient situations on the road.

Appliances and Equipment

As an integral part of pre-season checks, a detailed examination of all appliances and equipment within your RV is essential for a seamless travel experience.

Refrigerator

Run thorough checks on the refrigerator to ensure it is operating smoothly. Confirm that it's cooling efficiently and that the temperature settings are appropriate for preserving your food and beverages during your journey.

Stove

Examine the stove to verify that all burners are functioning correctly. This ensures that you can prepare meals efficiently while on the road, enhancing the overall convenience of your RV experience.

Microwave

Check the microwave for proper functioning. Ensure that it heats food evenly and that all controls are operational, providing you with a quick and convenient cooking option during your travels.

Water Heater

Inspect the water heater to guarantee it's in good working condition. A properly functioning water heater is essential for providing hot water and enhancing your comfort and convenience during showers and other water-related activities in your RV.

Safety Equipment

Ensuring the safety of your RV's occupants is paramount. Therefore, testing and verifying the functionality of safety devices is a critical step in pre-season checks.

Smoke Detectors and Carbon Monoxide Detectors

Test smoke detectors and carbon monoxide detectors to confirm that they are responsive and fully operational. These devices play a crucial role in providing early warnings and maintaining a safe environment within your RV.

Fire Extinguishers

Check fire extinguishers to ensure they are in good condition and have not expired. Replace batteries if needed, and confirm that the extinguisher is easily accessible in case of emergencies.

By diligently conducting these pre-season checks on HVAC, electrical, plumbing, appliances, and safety devices, you set the foundation for a worry-free and enjoyable RV travel experience.

Regular maintenance and attention to these crucial components contribute significantly to the overall reliability and safety of your RV.

Off-Season Prep

Preparing your RV for the off-season involves several crucial steps to ensure it remains in top condition during periods of inactivity, especially in the colder months.

Winterization

For RVs stored during the colder months, thorough winterization is indispensable. Start by completely draining the water system to prevent freezing, which can potentially lead to significant damage. Remove water from the pipes, tanks, and other components to mitigate the risk of expansion and rupture caused by freezing temperatures.

Following drainage, add antifreeze to plumbing lines and tanks. This serves as an additional safeguard against low temperatures. The antifreeze prevents residual water from freezing, offering a crucial layer of protection for your RV's plumbing system.

Protective Measures

Consider covering the RV or storing it in a sheltered area to shield it from harsh weather conditions, UV exposure, and debris. A cover provides an additional barrier against elements like snow, rain, and sunlight, safeguarding the exterior and preventing potential damage.

Ensuring proper ventilation is crucial during periods of inactivity to prevent mold or mildew growth. Good ventilation helps maintain a dry interior environment, reducing the risk of moisture-related issues. This is particularly important for preventing odors, stains, and damage to interior surfaces.

Battery Care

If your RV won't be in use for an extended period, consider disconnecting the battery to prevent drainage. This is especially relevant if the RV is not equipped with a battery disconnect switch. Disconnecting the battery helps preserve its charge during periods of inactivity.

Alternatively, if you prefer keeping the battery connected or if your RV has essential systems that require continuous power (like a security system or memory for electronic components), use a trickle charger. A trickle charger maintains a slow, steady charge, preventing the battery from losing its charge over time.

Engaging in regular seasonal maintenance practices, including comprehensive off-season preparation, is a fundamental approach to minimizing the risk of unexpected issues and ensuring the optimal condition of your RV. These steps contribute significantly to the overall quality and longevity of your RV, providing you with worry-free travel whenever you decide to embark on your adventures. Taking the time to properly prepare and care for your RV during off-season periods is an investment in its longevity and your future travel enjoyment.

HOW TO STORE YOUR RV OR CAMPING GEAR

Storing your RV and camping gear properly is crucial for preserving their longevity and ensuring they are ready for your next adventure.

RV Storage Guidelines

Weather Protection

For safeguarding your RV against the elements, consider either opting for a covered storage space or investing in a high-quality RV cover. This protective shield serves as a barrier against harsh weather conditions such as sunlight, rain, and snow, preventing damage to the exterior and helping maintain the paint and overall appearance.

Engine and System Maintenance

Before storing your RV, conduct a thorough pre-storage maintenance check. This includes inspecting the engine for signs of wear, leaks, or corrosion. Swiftly addressing any issues prevents potential deterioration during storage. Additionally, check fluid levels, such as oil, coolant, and brake fluid, to ensure they meet the manufacturer's recommendations. Verify tire pressure to avoid flat spots and preserve tire integrity. To prevent fuel system issues, consider using fuel stabilizers, which mitigate the impact of ethanol in the fuel, ensuring a smooth engine start when taken out of storage.

Interior Protection

To protect the interior of your RV during storage, initiate a thorough cleaning. Remove any dirt, dust, or residue from surfaces, appliances, and furniture. Declutter by eliminating perishable items, including food and toiletries, to deter pests. Open cabinets and drawers to promote ventilation, reducing the risk of mold or musty odors caused by trapped moisture.

Moisture Control

Moisture control is vital to prevent the growth of mold and mildew. Strategically place moisture-absorbing products, such as desiccants or moisture-absorbing crystals, inside the RV, focusing on areas prone to condensation to prevent the buildup of moisture.

Battery Care

Proper battery care is essential for ensuring your RV's battery remains functional when taken out of storage. Disconnect the battery to prevent drainage, or use a trickle charger to maintain a slow, steady charge. Store the disconnected battery in a cool, dry place, avoiding extreme temperatures that can impact its lifespan and performance.

By following these comprehensive guidelines, you not only protect your RV investment but also ensure it remains in optimal condition for your next adventure. Proper care during storage significantly contributes to the overall reliability and longevity of your next adventure. Proper care during storage significantly contributes to the overall reliability and longevity of your RV.

Camping Gear Storage Solutions

Moisture Control

Ensuring your camping gear stays dry is pivotal for preventing mold and odors. Before storage, meticulously clean and dry all items. Moisture-resistant storage containers or bags provide an additional layer of protection, shielding your gear from damp conditions that could compromise its integrity.

Cleaning Before Storage

Thoroughly cleaning and drying all camping equipment before storage is essential for its longevity. This includes tents, sleeping bags, cookware, and clothing. Tents, in particular, should be free of dirt and completely dry to prevent the growth of mildew, preserving their functionality and lifespan.

Organizing for Easy Access

Efficient organization simplifies future camping trips. Consider categorizing and storing camping gear in labeled containers for easy access. Group items such as cooking utensils, sleeping gear, and outdoor equipment to streamline the packing and unpacking process. Investing in storage racks or shelving units keeps items off the ground, aiding organization and accessibility.

Proper Ventilation

To prevent musty smells and maintain the freshness of your gear, proper ventilation is key. Store tents and sleeping bags in breathable storage bags or cotton sacks, allowing air circulation. This practice not only prevents odors but also contributes to the overall longevity of your camping equipment.

Secure Storage

Choosing a secure and controlled environment for gear storage is crucial. Opt for a location that minimizes the risk of theft or damage. This could involve a locked storage unit, a designated storage area in your home, or a secure garage. A controlled environment ensures your camping gear remains in top condition, ready for your next outdoor adventure.

Battery Maintenance

Proper battery maintenance is essential for ensuring your camping gear's battery remains in optimal condition for your outdoor adventures.

Charge the camping gear's batteries fully before storage. This ensures that the batteries are at their peak capacity when you're ready to use your camping equipment. A fully charged battery not only provides maximum power but also contributes to its overall longevity.

Periodically check and recharge the battery during extended storage to maintain its charge. Even in storage, batteries can slowly lose their charge over time. Regular checks and recharges prevent the battery from depleting completely, ensuring it's ready for use whenever you decide to embark on your next outdoor excursion.

Fuel System Care

Proper care of the fuel system is crucial, especially for camping stoves and lanterns, to avoid potential issues during storage.

For camping stoves and lanterns, empty fuel tanks before storage to prevent leaks. Storing equipment with empty fuel tanks minimizes the risk of fuel leakage and ensures a safer storage environment.

Ensure that propane tanks are turned off and their valves are closed securely to avoid any potential safety hazards. This precautionary measure not only prevents gas leaks but also safeguards against accidental ignition or other safety concerns.

Proper care during storage is an investment in the longevity and reliability of your outdoor equipment. When the time comes to venture into the great outdoors, you can do so with confidence, knowing that your camping gear is well-maintained and ready for your next adventure.

Guarding Against Unwanted Guests

It's not uncommon for the great outdoors or even when you're storing your camping goods to come with some uninvited guests, particularly in the form of rodents that might find their way into your RV or gear.

Investing in purpose-built rodent deterrent boxes is a straightforward approach. These boxes are designed to prevent rodents from accessing your RV or gear, providing a barrier against potential infestations. Placing these strategically around your camping area can act as an effective first line of defense.

For those who enjoy a touch of creativity and resourcefulness, a few bars of Irish Spring soap might be your unexpected ally in the battle against rodents.

Strategically place bars of Irish Spring soap in areas prone to rodent activity. This can include placing them in the corners of your RV, near potential entry points, or inside storage compartments. Rodents have a keen sense of smell, and the strong fragrance of Irish Spring soap is reputed to be a deterrent. The potent scent can act as a natural repellent, discouraging mice and other small critters from making your RV their temporary home.

This hack is not only cost-effective but also eco-friendly. Irish Spring soap is readily available and a relatively inexpensive solution compared to some commercial rodent repellents.

While Irish Spring soap is a popular choice, there may be other household items with scents that rodents find unpleasant. Some campers experiment with peppermint oil, cayenne pepper, or even fabric softener sheets as additional hacks to deter unwanted guests.

Being aware of the potential for rodents in your camping environment is the first step to a pest-free adventure. Whether you opt for purpose-built rodent deterrent boxes or get creative with household items like Irish Spring soap, the key is to stay vigilant. By incorporating these tricks into your camping routine, you can enjoy the great outdoors without worrying about unexpected guests seeking refuge in your RV or gear.

KEEPING YOUR CAMPSITE AND BELONGINGS SECURE

Think of your campsite security as your quiet companion, allowing you to enjoy the crackling campfire or explore nearby trails without that nagging worry about your stuff. It's like having the freedom to cook under the open sky or gaze at the stars, knowing your personal space is all good.

This feeling of security isn't just about things; it's about creating a vibe where you can truly connect with nature. Whether you're on a solo adventure, seeking peace, or sharing the experience with friends and family, a secure campsite turns your outdoor spot into a haven—a place where you can make memories, feel at home, and let the beauty of nature sink in.

Use of Locks

Investing in high-quality locks is your first line of defense against potential theft during your outdoor adventures. Opt for those that are durable and tamper-resistant, specifically designed for outdoor use to withstand varying weather conditions. Look for locks with hardened steel shackles for enhanced security.

Secure valuable items such as bikes, generators, and outdoor equipment with sturdy locks to deter theft. For larger items like bikes, consider using cable locks for their flexibility in securing irregular shapes. Loop the cable through frames or components and secure it tightly. Padlocks are ideal for securing storage compartments in your RV, adding an extra layer of protection to the contents within.

Alarms and Motion Sensors

Adding alarms and motion sensors to your campsite enhances its security by providing real-time alerts. Install these devices strategically, focusing on entry points and areas with valuable items. Opt for devices with adjustable sensitivity to minimize false alarms triggered by wildlife or natural movements.

Consider wireless alarms that communicate with a central control unit inside your RV or portable alarms that emit a loud sound when triggered. Some alarms are equipped with flashing lights to visually deter intruders. Explore alarms that can be integrated with smart camping systems, allowing you to receive alerts on your smartphone or other devices.

Strategic Placement of Items

Being mindful of where you place valuable items within your campsite contributes to its overall security. Refrain from leaving expensive gear in plain sight, especially when you're away from the campsite. Conceal valuables to minimize the temptation for opportunistic theft.

Store valuable items inside your RV or in securely locked storage compartments when not in use. This adds an extra layer of protection and keeps items out of sight. Plan the layout of your campsite to create a cozy and welcoming atmosphere, but ensure that valuable items are discreetly placed or secured.

By implementing these strategies, you significantly reduce the risk of theft and enhance the overall security of your campsite, allowing you to enjoy your outdoor experience with greater peace of mind.

Importance of Safety Measures

When it comes to outdoor adventures, prioritizing safety measures is non-negotiable. Here's a closer look at the importance of fire extinguishers, first aid kits, and emergency protocols.

Fire Extinguishers

Ensuring your campsite is equipped with functional fire extinguishers is a critical safety step. Always have a fire extinguisher easily accessible at your campsite, strategically placed for quick access in case of an emergency. Regularly check the pressure gauge to ensure it is in good working condition. If the pressure is below the recommended level, recharge or replace the extinguisher promptly. Educate yourself and fellow campers on the proper use of the fire extinguisher. Knowing how to operate it correctly is crucial during a fire emergency. Establish a designated meeting point for everyone to gather in case of emergencies. This ensures a quick and organized response to any potential threats.

First Aid Kits

A well-equipped first aid kit is your first line of defense against injuries and illnesses during your outdoor escapades. Maintain a comprehensive first-aid kit at your campsite, including various bandages, antiseptic wipes, pain relievers, and any necessary prescription medications. Regularly inspect the contents of the first aid kit and replenish any items that may have been used or have expired to ensure the kit is always ready for use.

Emergency Protocols

Establishing emergency protocols adds a layer of preparedness to your camping experience. Work with your camping companions to establish clear evacuation routes in case of emergencies. Familiarize yourself with multiple exit points and ensure everyone knows the plan. Share emergency contacts within the group and ensure everyone has this information readily available. Familiarize yourself with the campsite's emergency services, including the locations of fire extinguishers, emergency exits, and medical facilities. Research and identify the nearest medical facilities outside the campsite, as having this information can be crucial in cases of more severe emergencies.

Once you've solidified your grasp on campsite safety, including fire extinguishers, first aid kits, and emergency protocols, you can turn your attention to elevating your overall camping experience. Safety forms the foundation for unforgettable adventures, allowing you to explore the great outdoors with confidence and peace of mind.

In conclusion, maintaining, storing, and securing your RV and gear lays a solid foundation for a fulfilling camping lifestyle. As you become adept at these fundamental practices, you'll find yourself ready to explore more advanced techniques and fully enjoy the richness of the RV lifestyle. Consider this knowledge as the starting point for a deeper dive into advanced camping techniques. The next chapter will guide you toward unlocking more intricate aspects of RV living, providing you with the tools to savor an even more enriching outdoor experience.

CHAPTER 8

ADVANCED TIPS AND HACKS FOR SEASONED RVERS

Transitioning from a novice RVer to a seasoned traveler is like progressing from practicing scales on a musical instrument to composing a symphony. It's a journey marked by learning, adaptation, and a deepening connection with the nuances that transform RVing into an art form. This chapter serves as your guide to moving beyond the basics, inviting you to embark on a journey where expertise meets experience and the road becomes a canvas for your advanced RVing masterpiece.

As you transition from foundational RVing knowledge, you step into a realm where every curve of the road presents an opportunity for refined expertise. Embrace the nuances that elevate your travel experience, turning each trip into a carefully orchestrated adventure. From optimizing travel routes to mastering advanced RV maintenance, the landscape of possibilities expands as you delve into the intricacies of seasoned RVing.

Advanced RVers understand that the journey is as crucial as the destination. Beyond standard route planning, delve into sophisticated tools and apps providing real-time traffic updates, road conditions, and scenic detours. Navigate the open road with finesse, discovering hidden gems and avoiding unexpected pitfalls with the precision of a seasoned traveler.

No longer bound by novice uncertainties, seasoned RVers refine the art of campsite selection. Explore lesser-known sites and off-the-beaten-path locations where serenity meets the soul of true adventure. Advanced knowledge allows you to assess the amenities, surroundings, and unique features of each potential site, ensuring your chosen spot aligns seamlessly with your travel goals.

Elevate your RVing experience by mastering the art of energy efficiency. Advanced tips include solar panel installations, battery management systems, and energy-efficient appliances. Transform your RV into a self-sustaining haven, reducing your environmental footprint while extending your off-grid capabilities for an immersive and sustainable journey.

Seasoned RVers recognize the invaluable wealth of knowledge within the community. Engage in advanced strategies for community interaction, from joining specialized forums to attending advanced RVing events. Share experiences, learn from fellow travelers, and contribute to the collective wisdom that makes the RV community a dynamic and supportive network.

Transcend the generic travel itinerary and tailor your adventures to match your unique preferences. Advanced RVing involves customizing your journey, seeking out niche experiences, and immersing yourself in the local culture. Embrace spontaneity with a seasoned traveler's mindset, allowing for detours that transform your trip into an unforgettable tapestry of memories.

As you embark on this chapter of advanced tips and hacks, remember that RVing is not just a mode of travel; it's an evolving art form. Embrace the intricacies, fine-tune your approach, and let the road be your canvas as you paint a masterpiece of seasoned RVing expertise. The journey continues, and the possibilities are as boundless as the open road itself.

UPGRADING YOUR RV EXPERIENCE

Embarking on the journey of upgrading your RV is a thrilling step toward enhancing both comfort and functionality—from harnessing solar power to elevating your interior and integrating smart technology.

Solar Power Revolution

The decision to install solar panels on your RV is a transformative choice, extending beyond a mere nod to sustainable living; it marks a game-changer for off-grid adventures.

Solar power liberates you from dependence on traditional power outlets, offering a self-sufficient and renewable energy source. This newfound independence is particularly invaluable when exploring remote locations where access to electricity may be limited.

Solar panels harness the abundant energy from the sun, a renewable resource that ensures a continuous and sustainable power supply. This eco-friendly approach not only aligns with environmental consciousness but also allows for guilt-free exploration.

Embracing solar power contributes to a significant reduction in your carbon footprint. By relying on clean and renewable energy, you actively participate in minimizing the environmental impact of your RV travels.

Solar panels consist of photovoltaic cells that capture sunlight. These cells are made of semiconductor materials, typically silicon, which generate an electric current when exposed to sunlight.

When sunlight hits the solar panels, it excites electrons in the semiconductor material, creating an electric current. This current is then converted from direct current (DC) to alternating current (AC) by an inverter, making it compatible with your RV's electrical systems.

The generated electricity powers various onboard systems, including appliances, lights, and charging outlets. This means you can run your RV's essentials without relying on external power sources, offering flexibility and autonomy during your travels.

When choosing solar panels, consider the wattage to meet your energy needs. Higher-wattage panels generate more power, ensuring the efficient operation of your RV systems.

Optimal placement of solar panels is crucial for efficiency. Ensure the panels are positioned to receive maximum sunlight exposure throughout the day. This may involve tilting or adjusting the panels based on your location and the sun's trajectory.

Enhance your off-grid capabilities by integrating a quality battery storage system. This allows you to store excess energy generated during sunny periods for use during cloudy days or at night, ensuring a continuous power supply.

Embracing the solar power revolution for your RV not only brings tangible benefits in terms of energy independence and environmental responsibility but also opens up new possibilities for off-grid exploration, allowing you to venture further into nature without compromising on comfort and convenience.

Interior Overhaul

Embarking on an interior overhaul for your RV is a profound endeavor that transcends mere aesthetics; it's about sculpting a comfortable haven on wheels.

Investing in quality furnishings is paramount when revamping your RV's interior. The road poses unique challenges, and durable, well-built furniture is essential to withstand the rigors of constant travel. Opt for materials that are both comfortable and resilient, ensuring that your seating and sleeping areas remain inviting and intact throughout your journeys.

Upgrading appliances is a pivotal aspect of enhancing functionality within your RV. Modern, energy-efficient appliances not only contribute to a smoother travel experience but can also cater specifically to your needs. Consider appliances that align with your cooking preferences, storage requirements, and overall lifestyle. A well-equipped kitchen ensures that you can prepare meals effortlessly, adding a touch of home to your on-the-go lifestyle.

Infusing personalized decor brings a sense of identity and warmth to your mobile space. Select decor elements that resonate with your tastes and preferences, making the RV uniquely yours. This could include wall art, throw pillows, bedding, and other decorative items that not only reflect your personality but also contribute to a cozy and inviting atmosphere within the confines of your RV.

Creating a comfortable sleeping space is vital for a restful journey. Invest in a high-quality mattress that provides adequate support and comfort. Consider additional bedding elements like cozy blankets and soft pillows to enhance the overall sleep experience. A well-designed sleeping area transforms your RV into a sanctuary where you can unwind and recharge after a day of adventures.

The kitchen is the heart of any home, and the same holds true for your RV. Ensure your kitchen is well-equipped with appliances that cater to your culinary preferences. Consider storage solutions that maximize space and keep everything organized. A functional and well-stocked kitchen allows you to prepare meals with ease, fostering a sense of familiarity and homeliness on the road.

An interior overhaul for your RV is a holistic approach to creating a true home on wheels. By carefully selecting quality furnishings, upgrading appliances, infusing personalized decor, ensuring cozy sleeping arrangements, and optimizing your kitchen space, you not only enhance the functionality of your RV but also imbue it with a sense of comfort and identity. This transformation turns your RV into more than a mode of transportation—it becomes a haven that accompanies you on every journey, providing both solace and a touch of home wherever the road may lead.

Smart Technology Integration

The integration of smart technology into your RV represents a significant leap forward, offering a multitude of benefits in terms of functionality and security. Let's delve into the key aspects of incorporating smart technology to elevate your RV experience.

Enhance your comfort on the road by installing smart thermostats in your RV. These devices allow you to control the climate remotely, ensuring that your living space is at the perfect temperature upon your arrival. The ability to adjust heating or cooling settings through a mobile app adds a layer of convenience, allowing you to create a comfortable environment tailored to your preferences.

Investing in a security system equipped with smart features is a crucial step toward ensuring the safety of your RV. Smart security systems enable remote monitoring through your smartphone, offering real-time insights into your RV's surroundings. Features like motion detection, door/window sensors, and surveillance cameras contribute to comprehensive security, providing peace of mind whether you're inside the RV or exploring the outdoors.

Upgrade your RV's security infrastructure with smart locks and alarms. Smart locks offer keyless entry options, allowing you to lock and unlock your RV using a mobile app or code. This not only enhances convenience but also eliminates the risk of misplaced keys. Smart alarms provide an added layer of protection, alerting you instantly in the event of unauthorized access or any suspicious activity around your RV.

The seamless integration of these smart technologies not only adds a new level of convenience to your RV lifestyle but also significantly enhances overall safety. The ability to monitor and control various aspects of your RV remotely provides flexibility and peace of mind, allowing you to focus on enjoying your travels without constantly worrying about the security or climate control of your mobile home.

1. **Compatibility:** Ensure that the smart devices you choose are compatible with each other for seamless integration.
2. **Power source:** Consider the power requirements of the smart devices and ensure they align with your RV's electrical setup.

3. **Mobile connectivity:** Opt for devices that offer reliable mobile connectivity, allowing you to stay connected and in control wherever your travels take you.

By incorporating smart technology into your RV, you not only modernize your living space but also empower yourself with advanced tools for climate control and security. The integration of these technologies ensures that your RV becomes a smart, connected home on wheels, offering both convenience and peace of mind throughout your journeys.

Customization Tips

Customizing your RV is not just an upgrade; it's an opportunity to shape your mobile living space according to your preferences and needs. Let's delve into the intricacies of personalizing your RV with a focus on color schemes, storage solutions, and innovative space-saving furniture.

Choosing a color scheme sets the tone for your RV's interior ambiance. Opt for colors that resonate with your style and create a cohesive atmosphere. Lighter shades can make small spaces feel more open, while a carefully curated palette can evoke a specific mood. Consider the harmony between wall colors, upholstery, and decorative elements to craft a visually pleasing and inviting interior.

Effective storage solutions are essential to maximizing space utilization within your RV. Explore options that cater to the unique challenges of compact living. Utilize vertical spaces with tall cabinets and shelves, invest in storage bins or organizers that fit specific areas, and make use of under-bed or overhead storage compartments. Keeping your RV organized not only enhances visual appeal but also contributes to a clutter-free and functional living space.

Innovative space-saving furniture is a game-changer when it comes to optimizing the available square footage in your RV. Consider the following:

- **Folding tables:** These versatile tables can be set up when needed and folded away to create more space when not in use.
- **Collapsible chairs:** Opt for chairs that fold or collapse for easy storage, freeing up valuable floor space.
- **Modular storage options:** Invest in modular furniture with multi-functional features, such as beds with built-in storage or seating that doubles as storage compartments.

These space-saving furniture pieces are designed to ensure both functionality and comfort, allowing you to make the most of your limited living quarters without compromising on convenience or style.

1. **Personal preferences:** Prioritize features that align with your lifestyle and preferences.
2. **Multi-functional design:** Opt for furniture and decor that serves more than one purpose to maximize utility.
3. **Durability:** Choose materials that withstand the unique challenges of RV travel, ensuring longevity in various conditions.

By embracing customization, you transform your RV into a personalized haven that reflects your taste and caters to your practical needs. From thoughtfully chosen color schemes to innovative storage solutions and space-saving furniture, each element contributes to creating an inviting and functional living space on wheels. The customization process not only enhances the aesthetic appeal of your RV but also ensures that it becomes a true reflection of your unique style and preferences.

Quality Upgrades Matter

When considering upgrades for your RV, the emphasis should always be on quality. Each enhancement is not just an addition; it's an investment in the overall camping experience. Let's delve into why prioritizing durability, reliability, and reputable sources is crucial for a satisfying and enduring RV lifestyle.

Choosing durable materials for your RV upgrades is foundational to ensuring they withstand the challenges of the road. Whether it's furniture, flooring, or interior finishes, opt for materials known for their resilience. Robust materials not only endure the vibrations and movements during travel but also resist wear and tear over time. This longevity is key to maintaining the aesthetic appeal of your RV while ensuring a comfortable and reliable living space.

Investing in sturdy furniture is essential for both comfort and support. Quality seating and sleeping arrangements not only contribute to a comfortable living environment but also enhance the overall safety of your RV. Look for furniture built with strong frames and durable upholstery to withstand frequent use and movement.

When upgrading appliances, prioritize robustness and functionality. Appliances designed for the specific conditions of RV travel ensure reliable performance. From refrigerators to stoves, choose models known for their durability and efficiency. This ensures that your appliances not only enhance your camping experience but also stand the test of time.

For advanced technology upgrades, sourcing from reputable manufacturers is crucial. Whether it's smart thermostats, security systems, or other tech innovations, reputable brands offer reliability and seamless integration. Opting for established manufacturers ensures that you receive quality products backed by warranties and support, minimizing the risk of compatibility issues or premature failures.

Every upgrade represents an investment in the overall camping experience. Quality enhancements contribute to the longevity of your RV lifestyle, reducing the need for frequent replacements or repairs. The satisfaction derived from reliable and durable upgrades enhances the joy of travel, allowing you to focus on the adventure rather than worrying about the functionality of your RV.

Take the time to research materials, brands, and products to make informed decisions. While quality often comes with a higher price tag, consider it as a long-term investment in your RV's performance and your overall satisfaction.

By prioritizing quality in your RV upgrades, you not only enhance the functionality and comfort of your mobile living space but also contribute to the longevity and enjoyment of your RV lifestyle. Remember, each upgrade is a strategic investment in the durability and reliability of your RV, ensuring that it becomes a reliable and enjoyable companion on your journeys.

INNOVATIVE CAMPING HACKS

There are many different camping hacks that can make your trip even more enjoyable. Unfortunately, I cannot include all of them, so here is a look at five hacks that changed our camping experience.

Instant Foaming Hand Soap Hack

The Instant Foaming Hand Soap Hack is a clever and eco-friendly solution for maintaining hygiene in your RV. By repurposing a shampoo dispenser, you can effortlessly create instant foaming hand soap, minimizing waste and enhancing convenience.

Choose a dispenser with a pump mechanism, preferably one that dispenses foam. Opt for a gentle liquid hand soap of your choice, and distilled water is preferable, but any clean water will suffice.

Step-by-step instructions:

1. Ensure the shampoo dispenser is thoroughly cleaned and free of any residue from its previous use. Rinse it with water until no traces of shampoo remain.
2. If there is any remaining shampoo or liquid in the dispenser, empty it. This step is crucial to ensuring that the new hand soap remains uncontaminated.
3. In a separate container, mix the liquid hand soap with water. The ratio can vary, but a common recommendation is around 1 part soap to 2 parts water. Adjust the ratio based on your preference for soap concentration.
4. Carefully pour the diluted hand soap mixture into the shampoo dispenser. Be mindful not to overfill, leaving

enough space for the pump mechanism to work efficiently.

5. Test the foaming hand soap by pressing the pump. If the foam is too thick, add a bit more water. Conversely, if it's too thin, add a touch more liquid soap. Adjust until you achieve the desired consistency.

6. Secure the pump mechanism back onto the dispenser, ensuring it's tightly sealed to prevent leaks.

7. Consider labeling the dispenser to differentiate it from other cleaning products in your RV. This step is especially useful if you have multiple similar-looking containers.

Implementing the Instant Foaming Hand Soap Hack not only minimizes waste but also adds a touch of resourcefulness to your RV lifestyle. Enjoy the convenience of instant foam while contributing to a more sustainable and organized living space on the road.

Drip-Free Ice Pack

The Drip-Free Ice Pack is a simple yet ingenious hack to keep perishables cool without the mess. By freezing a saturated sponge in a ziplock bag, you create a reusable and mess-free ice pack for your RV adventures.

Choose a clean sponge that can fit comfortably inside a ziplock bag. Opt for a sponge with good absorbency for effective cooling. Select a sturdy and leak-proof ziplock bag that can accommodate the sponge without any risk of leaks.

Step-by-step instructions:

1. Thoroughly wet the sponge under a faucet or immerse it in water until it's completely saturated. Allow the sponge to absorb as much water as possible.

2. Gently squeeze the saturated sponge to remove any excess water. The goal is to have a damp but not dripping sponge.

3. Insert the damp sponge into the ziplock bag, ensuring it fits comfortably without causing the bag to overstretch.

4. Zip the bag securely, ensuring it's tightly sealed to prevent any leaks during freezing. Double-check the seal to avoid unwanted water in your freezer.

5. Place the sealed ziplock bag with the sponge in your freezer. Allow it sufficient time to freeze completely. Depending on the size of the sponge and your freezer settings, this typically takes a few hours.

6. Once frozen, take the ziplock bag out of the freezer and test the sponge's consistency. It should be firm and icy, ready to act as a reliable ice pack.

7. Place the Drip-Free Ice Pack in your cooler or refrigerator to keep perishables cool. The sponge will absorb any melting water, preventing it from creating a mess. After use, return the ice pack to the freezer for future cooling needs.

The Drip-Free Ice Pack is a practical and eco-friendly solution for keeping your perishables cool during your RV adventures. Enjoy the convenience of a reusable and mess-free cooling option that adds efficiency to your camping experience.

Shoe Organizer for Storage

This storage hack is a brilliant solution for optimizing the limited space in your RV. By repurposing a shoe organizer and hanging it over the bathroom door, you create a convenient storage space for toiletries and small items.

Choose a sturdy fabric or plastic shoe organizer with multiple pockets or compartments. The clear type is ideal for easy visibility of stored items. Ensure you have door hooks that are compatible with the thickness of your RV bathroom door. Over-the-door hooks are a suitable option.

- Choose a shoe organizer with a design that suits your needs. Look for one with varying pocket sizes to accommodate different items.
- Identify the ideal location over the bathroom door where the organizer will hang. Ensure it doesn't obstruct the door's movement.
- If your shoe organizer didn't come with hooks, attach door hooks to the top of the bathroom door. Make sure they are securely in place.
- Hang the shoe organizer on the door hooks. Adjust it to ensure it hangs evenly and securely.
- Utilize the pockets of the shoe organizer to store a variety of toiletries and small items. Consider categorizing items for easy access.
- Ensure the bathroom door can close securely without any hindrance from the hanging organizer.

The vertical storage solution makes use of otherwise unused space over the bathroom door. Clear pockets allow you to see the contents at a glance, making it easy to locate and access items.

Keep frequently used toiletries and small items within arm's reach, enhancing convenience during your RV travels. This hack doesn't involve any permanent modifications to your RV and can be easily removed if needed.

The shoe organizer for storage is a practical and space-saving solution for organizing toiletries and small items in your RV bathroom. Enjoy the benefits of a clutter-free and efficiently utilized space as you embark on your RV adventures.

Glow Stick Markers

This camping hack is a creative and efficient way to enhance safety during nighttime activities around your campsite. Whether you're camping in the wilderness or enjoying a night under the stars, these glow stick markers serve as practical indicators for tent stakes and potential trip hazards.

Acquire glow sticks of appropriate lengths and colors, considering the duration of the glow and the environmental conditions. Follow the instructions on the glow stick packaging to activate them. Typically, this involves bending the stick to break an inner capsule and shaking it to distribute the glowing solution.

Next, use string or twist ties to secure the glow sticks to tent stakes, guide ropes, or any potential trip hazards around the campsite. Ensure they are firmly attached. Strategically place the glow stick markers at key locations, emphasizing tent stakes and areas where people may walk during the night.

Once placed, test the visibility of the glow stick markers from different angles and distances to ensure they effectively illuminate the designated areas. Be aware of the expected glow duration of the chosen glow sticks; some may last for a few hours, providing ample coverage throughout the night.

The glow stick markers provide enhanced safety, significantly improving visibility and reducing the risk of tripping over tent stakes or obstacles in the dark. They are versatile and adaptable for different camping scenarios. Additionally, glow sticks offer a subtle and non-intrusive light, unlike bright flashlights or lanterns that may disturb the natural ambiance of the night.

It's essential to ensure the proper disposal of used glow sticks according to their packaging instructions and environmental guidelines. Enjoy the illuminated beauty of your surroundings while navigating safely during your outdoor adventures.

DIY Fire Starter Pods

Creating your own fire starter pods is a practical and efficient solution for ensuring reliable ignition for your campfire. This do-it-yourself (DIY) camping hack involves coating cotton pads in wax, providing a convenient and portable fire starter option. Here's a step-by-step guide to crafting these DIY Fire Starter Pods.

Choose high-quality, natural cotton pads or balls without synthetic additives. Opt for a wax that easily ignites and burns well. You'll also need a double boiler or microwave-safe bowl for melting the wax, tweezers or tongs to handle the cotton pads, and parchment paper or a non-stick surface for drying.

Step-by-step instructions:

1. Lay out parchment paper or a non-stick surface to place the coated cotton pads for drying.
2. If using a double boiler, melt the wax over low to medium heat. If using a microwave, melt the wax in a microwave-safe bowl according to the manufacturer's instructions.
3. Using tweezers or tongs, dip each cotton pad into the melted wax, ensuring it is fully coated. Alternatively, you can dip cotton balls.
4. Hold the coated cotton pad above the melted wax for a moment to allow the excess wax to drip off.
5. Carefully transfer the coated cotton pad to the prepared drying surface. Ensure it maintains its shape and does not stick to other pads.
6. Allow the coated cotton pads to dry completely. This may take a couple of hours, depending on the temperature and wax type.
7. Once dry, store the DIY Fire Starter Pods in a waterproof container to protect them from moisture during your camping trips.

By crafting your own DIY Fire Starter Pods, you ensure a hassle-free and efficient way to ignite your campfire, enhancing your overall camping experience with a reliable and portable fire-starting solution.

These creative hacks are designed to make your RVing experience more efficient and enjoyable. Experiment with these innovative solutions and discover how they can add convenience, sustainability, and a touch of resourcefulness to your adventures on the road. From streamlined hygiene practices to clever storage solutions, these hacks are your companions in creating a more comfortable and organized RV lifestyle.

ENGAGING WITH THE RV AND CAMPING COMMUNITY

Becoming an active member of the RV community adds a layer of richness to your journey, offering a supportive network of fellow enthusiasts. Here are some ways you can engage with the RV and camping communities.

1. Joining RV clubs

Consider becoming a member of RV clubs or organizations that resonate with your specific interests. These clubs often cater to diverse preferences, whether you're a solo traveler, a family, or someone seeking adventure-themed RV excursions. By joining, you tap into a community that shares your passion, providing opportunities for group travel, events, and shared resources.

2. Attending meetups and events

Participate in RV meetups, rallies, and events that bring enthusiasts together. These gatherings not only offer the chance to forge new friendships but also provide a platform for sharing experiences and discovering exciting destinations. Whether it's a local meetup or a larger rally, these events create a sense of camaraderie among RV enthusiasts.

3. Participating in forums

Engaging in online forums is a valuable way to connect with the broader RV community. Platforms like forums allow you to exchange knowledge, seek advice from experienced RVers, and stay updated on the latest trends and innovations. Whether you're troubleshooting technical issues, seeking travel recommendations, or sharing your own experiences, forums provide a virtual space to build connections and tap into collective wisdom.

The advantages of actively participating in the RV community extend beyond mere social interaction.

- **Camaraderie:** Experience a sense of camaraderie as you share the joys and challenges of RV life. Building connections with others who understand the unique aspects of RV travel creates a supportive community.
- **Insights and tips:** Gain valuable insights and tips from experienced RVers. Whether it's advice on maintenance, travel routes, or hidden gems, the collective knowledge within the community can significantly enhance your RVing experience.
- **Friendships:** Form lasting friendships with individuals who share your passion for the open road. These connections can lead to shared adventures, travel companionship, and a network of like-minded friends.

Engaging with the RV and camping community is not just about socializing; it's about tapping into a valuable resource of shared experiences and expertise. Whether you connect locally or virtually, the community provides a dynamic platform for growth, learning, and building connections that can last a lifetime.

EMBRACING LIFE ON THE ROAD

Embarking on the journey of full-time RV living is an exciting and complex endeavor that necessitates attention to both practical considerations and emotional adjustments.

Crucially, the establishment of a dependable mail forwarding service is essential to maintaining a connection with your permanent address. This service ensures the timely delivery of important documents, packages, and correspondence while you are on the road. It is advisable to select a service that aligns with your travel schedule and offers a secure means of receiving mail.

Ensuring access to reliable healthcare options is paramount for sustaining well-being on the road. This involves exploring health insurance plans that provide coverage across various locations and identifying healthcare providers that align with your travel routes, guaranteeing access to medical services when needed.

A pivotal aspect of transitioning to full-time RV living is the establishment of a sustainable income source. Whether through remote work, freelancing, or a mobile business, meticulous planning is essential to ensuring financial stability. Considering diversified income streams that can adapt to the nomadic nature of RV living is a prudent approach.

In terms of emotional considerations, maintaining relationships with friends and family becomes crucial. Leveraging technology for video calls, social media, and regular communication is instrumental. Additionally, planning visits and reunions is vital to strengthening connections despite geographical distances.

Constant travel brings both exhilarating moments of exploration and adventure, as well as challenges. Embracing these highs and lows requires developing resilience to navigate uncertainties, adapt to changing environments, and find joy in the unique experiences that come with life on the road.

Technology plays a crucial role in staying connected while on the road. Leveraging mobile hotspots, Wi-Fi signals at RV parks, and connectivity apps ensures seamless communication. Staying informed about available connectivity options at planned destinations is essential for maintaining consistent communication.

Optimizing connectivity involves investing in a reliable mobile hotspot device, considering a signal booster for enhanced connectivity in remote areas, and planning routes based on available cellular coverage to ensure a reliable internet connection. Exploring digital nomad-friendly workspaces that offer high-speed internet for remote work is an additional consideration.

Embracing life on the road requires a holistic approach that balances practical considerations with emotional well-being. By addressing both aspects, you can embark on a fulfilling journey of full-time RV living, enriched by meaningful connections and a profound sense of adventure.

As you reflect on the journey from beginner to seasoned RVer, remember that the adventure is ongoing. The possibilities in RVing are endless, filled with continuous learning, new adventures, and personal growth. The journey doesn't conclude here; it's an ever-evolving exploration of the open road.

As this chapter concludes, it's a reminder that the journey of RVing is not finite. Instead, it's a continuous cycle of discovery, where each mile traveled brings new lessons, each campground holds untold stories, and each sunrise marks the beginning of a fresh adventure.

SHARE YOUR STORIES!

I'd love to hear your camping stories, and they'll be a huge inspiration to new readers looking to get into the exciting world of camping and RVing. Here's a quick way for you to do that.

Simply by sharing your honest opinion of this book and a little about your own adventures, you'll show new readers where they can find all the guidance they need to set out on their own adventures.

MAKE A LASTING IMPRESSION!

Thank you so much for your support. A lifetime of freedom and adventure awaits!

CONCLUSION

Embarking on the camping journey, whether nestled in a tent beneath the stars or cruising the open roads in an RV, marks a profound transformation. From the early days of being a camping novice to evolving into a seasoned traveler, the experience is a continual learning curve, extending beyond mastering the basics to truly embracing the artistry of RVing.

The underlying message resonating throughout this exploration is the encouragement to wholeheartedly embrace the limitless possibilities that unfold within the realm of RVing. Each road trip serves as a blank canvas, and you, the adventurer, wield the paintbrush, crafting unique and indelible experiences along the winding pathways of your travels.

As you absorb the wisdom and confidence derived from the insights within these pages, the time has come to step boldly onto your personal odyssey. Recognize that every journey is a narrative waiting to be penned, encouraging you to savor each moment, share your stories with fellow travelers, and continually learn and grow amidst the perpetual tapestry of adventures that await.

Your feedback, a precious contribution to the collective journey, is sincerely valued. Consider taking a moment to leave a review, sharing your own camping adventures. Your experiences have the potential to inspire and connect you with a broader community of kindred spirits. May your future travels be safe, exhilarating, and filled with the joy of discovery!

BONUS CHECKLIST

Having a comprehensive checklist before hitting the road with an RV or a camper, especially for travel trailers, is crucial for a safe and smooth journey. Here is a checklist you can use before hitting the road.

1. Check Tires:

Inspect each tire for proper inflation using a pressure gauge. Look for any visible signs of damage, such as bulges, cuts, or excessive wear.

2. Secure Loose Items:

Walk through the interior of the RV to ensure that all loose items, such as dishes, appliances, or personal belongings, are securely stowed. Use non-slip mats or other securing methods if needed.

3. Close and Lock Windows and Doors:

Verify that all windows and doors are fully closed and securely locked. This includes cabinets and drawers inside the RV.

4. Check Hitch Components:

Examine the hitch components, including the receiver, ball mount, and any weight distribution or sway control systems, for signs of wear, rust, or damage. Ensure all bolts and connections are tight.

HOOK UP TO TRAILER

1. Inspect Coupler and Ball:

Examine the coupler on the trailer and the hitch ball on the tow vehicle. Ensure there is no rust, damage, or debris. Clean as needed for a secure connection.

2. Lock Ball and Insert Cotter Pin:

Lock the hitch ball into the coupler and secure it with the locking mechanism. Insert the cotter pin through the locking mechanism to prevent accidental unlocking.

3. Connect Electronic Brake Controller:

If your RV has electric brakes, connect the electronic brake controller in the tow vehicle to the trailer. Adjust settings based on the trailer's weight.

4. Attach Safety Chains:

Cross the safety chains beneath the hitch and connect them to the designated attachment points on the tow vehicle. Ensure they are not dragging on the ground.

5. Connect Emergency Brake Cable:

Attach the emergency brake cable from the trailer to the tow vehicle. This is a backup in case the trailer becomes detached.

6. Secure Breakaway Switch:

If your RV has a breakaway switch, ensure it is securely attached to the tow vehicle. The breakaway switch activates the trailer brakes if it detaches from the tow vehicle.

7. Install Sway Control Devices:

If using anti-sway bars or weight distribution systems, follow the manufacturer's instructions for proper installation. Ensure they are securely attached and locked in place.

LIGHTS AND SIGNALS

1. Test Brake Lights and Turn Signals:

Have a helper assist you in testing all the lights on the trailer, including the brake lights, turn signals, and running lights. Replace any bulbs that are not functioning.

2. Activate Wireless Rear Camera:

If your RV is equipped with a wireless rear camera, turn it on and adjust the angle to provide clear visibility of the trailer while driving.

FINAL CHECKS:

1. Double-Check Hitch Locks:

Confirm that all hitch components, including coupler locks and any other locking mechanisms, are securely in place.

2. Verify Trailer Brake Operation:

Test the trailer brakes by applying the brake controller in the tow vehicle. Ensure that the trailer brakes engage smoothly.

3. Adjust Mirrors:

Adjust the side mirrors on the tow vehicle to provide optimal visibility of the trailer and surrounding traffic.

4. Review Route and Stops:

Take a final look at your planned route, noting any potential challenges such as construction zones or narrow roads. Identify rest stops or gas stations for planned breaks.

By carefully going through these steps, you enhance the safety and efficiency of your RV towing setup, contributing to a smoother and more enjoyable journey. Safe travels!

REFERENCES

Akpan, K. (2021, November 18). *How to create a budget for RV life*. Camping World Blog. https://blog.campingworld.com/learn-to-rv/how-to-create-a-budget-for-rv-life/

Alyssa. (2023, July 27). *Expert RVers reveal 33+ best camper hacks & tips*. Fulfilling Travel. https://www.fulfillingtravel.com/best-camper-hacks/

Beach camping: the best spots, the best tips. (2020, July 15). Johnson Outdoors. https://eurekacamping.johnsonoutdoors.com/us/blog/beach-camping

Bennett, M. (2020, October 21). *The real cost of RV ownership. Here's what we spent*. RV Love. https://rvlove.com/planning/the-real-cost-of-rv-ownership-heres-what-we-spent/

Bressler, S. (2019, November 7). *9 Essential tips to rock overnight parking your RV*. The Crazy Outdoor Mama. https://www.thecrazyoutdoormama.com/9-essential-tips-to-rock-overnight-parking-your-rv/

Brittany. (2019, October 19). *Ultimate RV trip planner: A guide to planning your RV road trip*. The Rolling Pack. https://therollingpack.com/ultimate-rv-trip-planner-a-guide-to-planning-your-rv-road-trip/

Campendium. (2023, June 9). *Tools of the road: essentials for your RV toolkit*. Campendium. https://go.campendium.com/rv-tool-box/

Camping safety tips for setting up a safe campsite. (2023, July 28). State Farm. https://www.statefarm.com/simple-insights/auto-and-vehicles/simple-tips-for-camping-safety

Dennis, C. (2023, April 21). *20 Best travel trailer & RV decorating ideas (Easy to do!)*. The DIY Mommy. https://thediymommy.com/best-travel-trailer-rv-decorating-ideas-easy-to-do/

Do It Yourself RV. (2023, August 17). *RV upgrades that add value: What's worth investing in?* https://www.doityourselfrv.com/rv-upgrades-that-add-value/

Ethans, L. (2021, August 15). *Key features to consider before buying a tent*. BackyardBoss; BackyardBoss. https://www.backyardboss.net/key-features-to-consider-before-buying-a-tent/

Eyton, T. (2018, October 11). *How to leave no trace (and why it's important!)*. Happiest Outdoors. https://happiestoutdoors.ca/how-to-leave-no-trace/

Falin, L. (2023, May 30). *How to find the best RV deals.* RVshare. https://produc
tion-blog.rvshare.com/how-to-find-the-best-rv-deals/

15 campground etiquette rules everyone should follow. (2019, September 20).
WPLG.   https://www.local10.com/travel/2019/09/20/15-campground-
etiquette-rules-everyone-should-follow/

4 Tips for choosing safe rest stops when traveling. (2022, January 16). Hurst Towing
and Recovery. https://hursttowing.com/choosing-safe-rest-stops-when-travel
ling/

14 Camping safety tips for the great outdoors. (2021). Koa.com. https://koa.com/
blog/14-camping-safety-tips-for-the-great-outdoors/

Gaedtke, R. (2022, April 19). *How to choose a camping tent.* GearLab; GearLab.
https://www.outdoorgearlab.com/topics/camping-and-hiking/best-camping-
tent/buying-advice

Genter, J. (2022, November 22). *The best RV rental companies and how to choose.*
NerdWallet. https://www.nerdwallet.com/article/travel/rv-rental-companies-
best

Gonzales, C. (2020, August 2). *7 Ways to optimize space in your new RV.* Do It
Yourself RV. https://www.doityourselfrv.com/new-rv-organization/

Gonzales, C. (2021, March 29). *The different types of RV camping.* RVshare.
https://rvshare.com/blog/types-of-rv-camping/

Guinan, K. (2024, January 12). *Renting vs. buying an RV: Which option makes the
most sense?* Bankrate; Bankrate.com. https://www.bankrate.com/loans/
personal-loans/should-you-buy-or-rent-an-rv/#renting

Headley, L. (2023, August 4). *The 5 Best RV GPS systems for safe and smooth traveling.* Beyond the Tent. https://www.beyondthetent.com/best-rv-gps/

How did you guys get into camping? (2022). Reddit.com. https://www.reddit.com/
r/camping/comments/vtexi6/how_did_you_guys_get_into_camping/

How much Is an RV to rent, buy, or resell? (2023, April 21). TAXA Outdoors.
https://taxaoutdoors.com/blogs/articles/how-much-is-an-rv-to-rent-buy-or-resell

How to choose your camping gear? (2021, October 5). Quechua.com. https://www.
quechua.com/how-to-choose-your-camping-gear

How to hook up sewer on a travel trailer. (2021). J.D. Power. https://www.jdpower.
com/rvs/shopping-guides/how-to-hook-up-sewer-on-a-travel-trailer

Jul3s. (2020, November 11). *Important factors to consider when choosing your
campsite.* Here We Tow. https://www.herewetow.co.uk/important-factors-to-
consider-when-choosing-your-campsite/

Knight, M. (2020, March 30). *Top 5 RV mods and upgrades.* Adventurous Way.
https://www.adventurousway.com/blog/top-5-rv-mods-upgrades

Koberg, K. (2020, May 22). *First-time RV setup checklist: A step-by-step user's guide*. RV Jack Pads. https://rvjackpads.com/first-time-rv-setup-a-step-by-step-users-guide/

Lawrence, E. (2023, June 15). *Power outages at RV parks: What you need to know*. Do It Yourself RV. https://www.doityourselfrv.com/power-outage-camp ground/

Leave no trace of seven principles. (2024). REI; REI. https://www.rei.com/learn/expert-advice/leave-no-trace.html

Maunakea, M. (2019, July 2). *Beginner's guide: How to select a good campsite*. Huck Adventures. https://huckadventures.com/how_to_select_a_good_camp site/

Mike. (2023, August 19). *9 Steps to Budgeting for unforgettable RV adventures!* Our Campfire Unplugged. https://ourcampfireunplugged.com/9-steps-to-budgeting-for-unforgettable-rv-adventures/

Morton, T., & Morton, C. (2022, January 23). *Top 10 easily missed things to look for when buying an RV*. Mortons on the Move. https://www.mortonsonthe move.com/things-to-look-for-when-buying-an-rv/

Murden, D. (2022, June 16). *How long do motorhomes last- average lifespan for each class*. Oaktree Motorhomes. https://omcmotorhomes.co.uk/how-long-do-motorhomes-last/

Must have features for your RV (2020, January 9). Hilltop Camper & RV Blog. https://www.hilltopcamper.com/blog/must-have-features-for-your-rv/

Pitching the perfect tent: A guide to choosing the right camping tent size for your needs. (2023, April 11). Camp and Climb. https://campandclimb.co.za/blog/pitching-the-perfect-tent-a-guide-to-choosing-the-right-camping-tent-size-for-your-needs

Plan for the weather on your next camping or RV trip – Visual Crossing Weather. (2021, May 10). Visual Crossing Weather. https://www.visualcrossing.com/resources/blog/plan-for-the-weather-on-your-next-camping-or-rv-trip/

Pryse, M. (2022, August 18). *7 Key tent features to consider in your next purchase*. Camping Australia; Camping Australia. https://campingaustralia.com.au/blogs/expert-advice/7-key-tent-features-to-consider-in-your-next-purchase

Puglisi, J. (2021, July 22). *6 Best navigation apps for RVing*. This Is Go RVing. https://www.gorving.com/tips-inspiration/expert-advice/6-best-navigation-apps-rving

Randall, M. (2019, July 3). *A guide to do-it-yourself RV water supply systems*. Your RV Lifestyle. https://www.your-rv-lifestyle.com/rv-water-supply-systems/

Rapier, G. (2019, June 6). *11 things you should always look for when buying an RV*.

Business Insider; Insider. https://www.businessinsider.com/buying-an-rv-tips-advice-what-to-look-out-for-2019-6

Region 5 - Outdoor safety & ethics. (2024). USDA Forest Service. https://www.fs.usda.gov/detail/r5/recreation/safety-ethics/?cid=stelprdb5365666#:

Rivera, H. (2024, January 19). *Getting an RV loan.* Bankrate; Bankrate.com. https://www.bankrate.com/loans/personal-loans/how-to-qualify-for-an-rv-loan/#qualify

Robinson, D. (2022, June 30). *Best RV loans, rates, and financing terms.* Market Watch Guides; MarketWatch. https://www.marketwatch.com/guides/car-loans/best-rv-loans/

Russo, J. (2023, February 13). *20 Must-have tools for your RV tool kit - are you carrying these tools?* We're the Russos. https://weretherussos.com/must-have-tools-rv-tool-kit/

RV essentials list for newbies: The gear you never want to forget. (2021, August 26). Heartland RVs. https://heartlandrvs.com/rv-essentials-for-newbies-the-gear-you-never-want-to-forget/

RV guide: Types of RVs. (2018). Generalrv.com. https://www.generalrv.com/blog/rving-101-rv-types/

RV living: What's fueling the changing RV landscape. (2024). Progressive.com. https://www.progressive.com/resources/insights/living-in-an-rv/

RV ownership costs: How much does it cost to own? (2018). Koa.com. https://koa.com/blog/the-beginners-guide-to-buying-an-rv-understanding-ownership-costs/

RV types - Learn more about your options and the different types of RVs available. (2024). The ZaneRay Group. https://www.thorindustries.com/rv-types

RV types 101: What to know about each category of RV. (2021, July 8). Heartland RVs. https://heartlandrvs.com/rv-types-101-what-to-know-about-each-category-of-rv/

RV Wholesale Superstore. (2023, January 16). *RV emergency preparedness tips for safer trips.* https://www.rvwholesalesuperstore.com/learn/rv-emergency-preparedness-tips/

Shivani. (2018, February 19). *5 Tips for choosing a campsite in a forest.* The Wandering Core. https://thewanderingcore.com/5-tips-campsites-how-to-choose-a-campground-in-forest-guest-post/

Sedano, Isabela. "40 Camping Quotes and Sayings to Enjoy the Great Outdoors." TRVST. Last modified August 12, 2023. https://www.trvst.world/mind-body/camping-quotes/

Shorr, T. (2022, September 12). *6 Practical money-saving tips for RV travel.*

Unique RV Camping with Harvest Hosts; Harvest Hosts. https://harvesthosts. com/rv-camping/practical-rv-travel-money-saving-tips/

6 tips for easy setup tents. (2023). Https://Www.pomoly.com. https://www. pomoly.com/6-Tips-for-Easy-Set-Up-Tents-a709789.html

Skylis, M. B. (2023, May 2). Road ready: Six ways to optimize RV space. Blue Ridge Outdoors Magazine. https://www.blueridgeoutdoors.com/camping/road-ready-six-ways-to-optimize-rv-space/

Spike, D. (2023, June 12). The benefits of RV camping over traditional tent camping. Campmart.ca. https://www.campmart.ca/blog/the-benefits-of-rv-camping-over-traditional-tent-camping--58367

Storgaard, M. (2022, July 27). Where Is my RV leaking? 3 Quick troubleshooting tips. Go Downsize; Go Downsize. https://www.godownsize.com/where-is-my-rv-leaking-tips/

Stress-free camping storage ideas for organizing camping gear. (2021, June 28). Take the Truck. https://www.takethetruck.com/blog/camping-storage-ideas

10 camping essentials & must-haves list. (2023, April 25). Johnsonoutdoors.com. https://eurekacamping.johnsonoutdoors.com/us/blog/10-essential-camping-items

The 7 principles. (2023, September 6). Leave No Trace. https://lnt.org/why/7-prin ciples/

The advantages of renting an RV vs. buying. (2023, June 13). HPRV. https://www. hightenedpath.com/blogs/the-advantages-of-renting-an-rv-vs-buying/

The history of RV camping and how to care for yours. (2024). Petroleum Service Company. https://petroleumservicecompany.com/blog/rv-camping-history/

The Transwest Team. (2022, September 15). RV hookups explained: Electricity, water, sewage, & TV. Transwest; Transwest RVs. https://www.transwest.com/ rv/blog/rv-hookups-explained-electricity-water-sewage-and-tv/#:

Turning radius planning. (2021). Keystone RV Forums. https://www.keystonefo rums.com/forums/showthread.php?t=46003

Types of tents: 17 popular tent styles for camping and backpacking. (2020, November 17). Outdoors Cult. https://www.outdoorscult.com/types-of-tents/

Waddington, E. (2019, February 7). RV energy saving tips. Your RV Lifestyle. https://www.your-rv-lifestyle.com/rv-energy-saving-tips/

Wendland, M. (2022, November 25). RV hookups for beginners (5 steps for your first trip). RV Lifestyle. https://rvlifestyle.com/rv-hookups-for-beginners/

Wendland, M. (2023, June 9). Slow down! 5 Reasons RVers should take it slow. RV Lifestyle. https://rvlifestyle.com/take-it-slow/

What are the biggest problems RV owners face? | Inland Truck Parts & Service.

(2019). Inlandtruck.com. https://www.inlandtruck.com/who-we-are/from-the-experts/2019/10/25/what-are-the-biggest-problems-rv-owners-face

What to consider when choosing an RV campground. (2024). Www.granddesignrv.com. https://www.granddesignrv.com/adventure-more/live/what-to-consider-when-choosing-an-rv-campground

Why do you RV? (2023). Reddit.com. https://www.reddit.com/r/GoRVing/comments/y6r28d/why_do_you_rv/

Wollenhaupt, G. (2023, July 21). *How to finance an RV.* LendingTree. https://www.lendingtree.com/auto/rv/how-to-finance-an-rv/

You may find some hidden or surprising expenses that come with owning an RV. (2021, March 22). Transparency Insurance Services. https://www.transparityinsurance.com/what-is-true-cost-rv-ownership/

Your RV Good Guide. (2023). *The ultimate guide to cleaning and caring for your motorhome.* RV Super Centre. https://www.rvsupercentre.co.nz/blog/our-blog/buyer-guides/the-ultimate-guide-to-cleaning-and-caring-for-your/

IMAGE REFERENCES

Andrew Main Oster. (2023, February 4). *Waterfall seen from tent · free stock photo.* Pexels. https://www.pexels.com/photo/waterfall-seen-from-tent-15310519/

Belogor. (2018, August 16). *Beach sand tent.* Pixabay. https://pixabay.com/photos/beach-sand-tent-vacation-tourism-3604912/

Bertelli, M. (2018, January 13). *Blue ceramic mug.* Pexels. https://www.pexels.com/photo/blue-ceramic-mug-799445/

Chulmin1700. (2020, March 2). *Spring vacation camping early.* Pixabay. https://pixabay.com/photos/spring-vacation-camping-4891823/

Elliott, T. (2021, February 18). *A car with a tent on top.* Pexels. https://www.pexels.com/photo/a-car-with-a-tent-on-top-6861136/

HLS 44. (2021, May 20). *White and blue camper trailer on green grass field during daytime.* Unsplash. https://unsplash.com/photos/white-and-blue-camper-trailer-on-green-grass-field-during-daytime-SGEBKQQoLNk

ITUBB. (2021a, January 8). *Tent camping outdoors.* Pixabay. https://pixabay.com/photos/tent-camping-outdoors-campground-5887142/

ITUBB. (2021b, December 24). *Camping tent night.* Pixabay. https://pixabay.com/photos/camping-tent-night-camping-campfire-6882479/

Kim, S. (2020, March 16). *Orange and gray dome tent on a green grass field near a body of water during daytime.* Unsplash. https://unsplash.com/photos/orange-

and-gray-dome-tent-on-green-grass-field-near-body-of-water-during-daytime-LMwIIIGsFSg

Lukas. (2018, August 10). *Tents on the ground.* Pexels. https://www.pexels.com/photo/tents-on-the-ground-1309587/

Memory Catcher. (2020a, April 10). *Motorhome camper mobile.* Pixabay. https://pixabay.com/photos/motorhome-camper-mobile-camping-5024832/

Memory Catcher. (2020b, April 28). *Camping motorhome traveling.* Pixabay. https://pixabay.com/photos/camping-motorhome-traveling-camper-5099382/

Mike Goad. (2019, February 17). *Truck camper stop action blur.* Pixabay. https://pixabay.com/photos/truck-camper-stop-action-blur-truck-4003106/

Paulbr75. (2016, August 24). *Old restored camper recreation.* Pixabay. https://pixabay.com/photos/old-restored-camper-recreation-1617518/

Robert Forever Ago. (2019, June 19). *Photo of a person standing near the cliff edge.* Pexels. https://www.pexels.com/photo/photo-of-person-standing-near-cliff-edge-2496880/

Roy, S. (2020, July 28). *People sit on camping chairs near green tents during the daytime.* Unsplash. https://unsplash.com/photos/people-sitting-on-camping-chairs-near-green-tent-during-daytime-BmUW6ypOgU8

Shuraeva, A. (2020, October 3). *Tent with a table on a wooden floor in the forest.* Pexels. https://www.pexels.com/photo/tent-with-table-on-wooden-floor-in-forest-4989512/

Sreehari Devadas. (2020, May 27). *People sit on camping chairs near tents during the daytime.* Unsplash. https://unsplash.com/photos/people-sitting-on-camping-chairs-near-tent-during-daytime-G5n5AC6CcoY

Wellington, J. (2017, September 26). *RV camper night.* Pixabay. https://pixabay.com/photos/rv-camper-night-camping-adventure-2788677/

Yesmir. (2022, July 12). *Camping teepee tent tenpung.* Pixabay. https://pixabay.com/photos/camping-teepee-tent-tenpung-7315405/